the arc

the arc

A Formal Structure for a Palestinian State

DOUG SUISMAN

STEVEN N. SIMON

GLENN E. ROBINSON

C. ROSS ANTHONY

MICHAEL SCHOENBAUM

Supported by a gift from Guilford Glazer

The research described in this report was initiated by Guilford Glazer and funded by his generous gift. This research in the public interest was also supported by RAND, using discretionary funds made possible by RAND's donors and earnings on client-funded research. This research was conducted under the direction of the RAND Center for Middle East Public Policy (CMEPP), a unit of the RAND Corporation.

Library of Congress Cataloging-in-Publication Data
The arc : a formal structure for a Palestinian state / Doug Suisman ... [et al.].
     p. cm.
     "MG-327."
     Includes bibliographical references.
     ISBN 0-8330-3770-6 (pbk. : alk. paper)
     1. Arab-Israeli conflict—1993– —Peace. 2. Newly independent states. 3. Palestine—
Economic conditions. 4. Palestine—Social conditions. 5. Palestine—Politics and
government. I. Suisman, Douglas R.
     DS119.76.A74 2005
     307.3'095695'3—dc22

                                       2005005999

THE RAND CORPORATION IS A NONPROFIT RESEARCH ORGANIZATION PROVIDING OBJECTIVE ANALYSIS AND EFFECTIVE SOLUTIONS THAT ADDRESS THE CHALLENGES FACING THE PUBLIC AND PRIVATE SECTORS AROUND THE WORLD. RAND'S PUBLICATIONS DO NOT NECESSARILY REFLECT THE OPINIONS OF ITS RESEARCH CLIENTS AND SPONSORS. RAND® IS A REGISTERED TRADEMARK.

Cover and book design by Ph.D, www.phdla.com

Printed on New Leaf Reincarnation Matte, made with 100% recycled fiber, 50% post-consumer waste and processed chlorine free.

PUBLISHED 2005 BY THE RAND CORPORATION
1776 MAIN STREET, P.O. BOX 2138, SANTA MONICA, CA 90407-2138
1200 SOUTH HAYES STREET, ARLINGTON, VA 22202-5050
201 NORTH CRAIG STREET, SUITE 202, PITTSBURGH, PA 15213-1516
RAND URL: http://www.rand.org/
TO ORDER RAND DOCUMENTS OR TO OBTAIN ADDITIONAL INFORMATION, CONTACT
DISTRIBUTION SERVICES: TELEPHONE: (310) 451-7002;
FAX: (310) 451-6915; EMAIL: order@rand.org

Preface

IN 2003, THE RAND CORPORATION was approached by a donor who was concerned that a large-scale return of refugees to a Palestinian state would destabilize the new entity and perpetuate conditions that had engendered decades of violence between Palestinians and Israelis and among Palestinians themselves. The donor also expressed a conviction that Palestinian militant groups, especially Hamas, might be induced to work constructively toward successful statehood and peace with Israel if the group's leadership and supporters had a tangible vision of the benefits of peace. This combination of anxiety and hope led him to ask RAND to explore resettlement possibilities for Palestinians in the aftermath of a final status accord with Israel.

In keeping with his insight into the inspiring power of symbols, the donor proposed that RAND focus particularly on the potential of a new city that would be dedicated to accommodating the influx of Palestinian refugees and, 50 years after exile, their many descendants. The donor is a builder, so his instinctive approach might have been expected to lean in this direction. Nonetheless, the image of a new city is a potent one in the American imagination. In 1630, upon landing at Plymouth, John Winthrop declared to members of the assembled Puritan community that they "shall be as a city upon a hill" and a beacon unto the nations. He was drawing on the New Testament[1], not the Qur'an, but the image is nevertheless strikingly apt, since Winthrop's Gospel source drew on an older biblical tradition that portrayed Shemer—the eponymous Samarian city—as the city on a hill.[2] And Shemer is the ancient Semitic name for the northern West Bank, a large part of the territory that will constitute a Palestinian state.

In accepting the donor's challenge, RAND set out to develop a range of planning options, both for reasons of analytical completeness and a sense that a single new mega-city, despite its poetic virtue, might not be economically, logistically, or environmentally feasible. Yet throughout this process, we sought an urban and infrastructural solution that would embody the iconic power that would dramatize the emergence of a new independent state. Our research objective, therefore, was not simply to develop a concept for housing refugees, but also to offer a vision that would inspire all Palestinians, regardless of their place of birth or current residence. The authors also strove to develop a concept that might be implemented in stages so that work might begin even before Palestine had achieved independence, thereby providing the tangible, transforming hope of a better life that might spur intra-Palestinian cooperation. The project sponsor emphasized to us that there is no one more dangerous than a person without hope.

RAND was well-equipped to carry out this project. At the time the donor for this project approached RAND, we were wrapping up a broad-gauged analysis of the full range of issues that Palestinians and their international partners would have to address to ensure that the new state succeeded. Thus, the RAND team had already carried out detailed research, including fact-finding trips to Palestine, on topics essential to the present book, especially demographics, resources, economics, and governance. Although it is not necessarily obvious, the work presented here depends to a significant degree on this analytical spadework. RAND's earlier study is described in *Building a Successful Palestinian State* (The RAND Palestinian State Study Team, 2005).

For the design component of the current undertaking, RAND partnered with Suisman Urban Design, which contributed to a new vision plan for Lower Manhattan in the wake of 9/11 (through the Regional Plan Association), developed the master plan for the Los Angeles Civic Center, designed the Metro Rapid bus system for the Los Angeles County Metropolitan Transit Authority, and is now working on master plans for First Street and for Grand Avenue in downtown Los Angeles. Although the firm had not worked in the region, it consulted with regional experts. More importantly, however, the designers were able to bring an urban focus to the project by conceiving of a Palestinian state as a single metropolitan region requiring both physical and economic integration. Beginning with the region's existing topography and the state's projected size and population, our design partners proceeded to generate a new structural concept for future settlement, open space, and infrastructure. The result is a vision we refer to as the Arc, which we describe in this book.

The Arc is an idea meant to stimulate thinking about infrastructure designs that would best meet the needs of a rapidly growing Palestinian state. It is a concept, not a plan. Such a plan could emerge only from vigorous, inclusive debate within the community of Palestinians. RAND's intention was to contribute to this debate rather than prefigure its outcome. The authors are dedicated to the proposition that there are multiple right answers and what ultimately matters is the consensus of Palestinians on preferred infrastructural forms, not the convictions of outsiders, regardless of the quality of their intentions.

This work should be of interest to the Israeli and Palestinian communities; to Palestinian government officials; to policymakers in the Roadmap Quartet (the United States, the European Union, the United Nations, and Russia); to foreign policy experts; and to organizations and individuals committed to helping establish and sustain a successful state of Palestine. It should also be of interest to the negotiating teams charged with the responsibility of establishing the new state.

The Arc: A Formal Structure for a Palestinian State was initiated by Guilford Glazer and funded by his generous gift. This research in the public interest was also supported by RAND, using discretionary funds made possible by the generosity of RAND's other donors and the earnings on client-funded research. The research was conducted under the direction of the RAND Center for Middle East Public Policy (CMEPP), a unit of the RAND Corporation.

---

[1] Matthew 5:14.

[2] "He bought the hill of Samaria from Shemer for two talents of silver and built a city on the hill, calling it Samaria, after Shemer, the name of the former owner of the hill" (1 Kings 16:24).

Acknowledgments

MANY PEOPLE BOTH WITHIN AND OUTSIDE OF RAND contributed to this book. The Arc concept was developed from the conclusions and recommendations of the companion volume, *Building a Successful Palestinian State*. The authors are deeply indebted to the authors of that study and to the numerous Palestinian and Israeli experts who graciously donated their time and expertise to provide source material.

We are equally indebted to Robert Lane of the Regional Plan Association, who contributed key insights and concepts to the project and who, along with Robert Yaro, reviewed it at numerous stages. They helped shape the scope and scale of the project. We would also like to acknowledge with gratitude the influence of Professor Klaus Herdeg in his development of the concept of formal structure.

The authors would also like to thank the staff of Suisman Urban Design, including Helen Choi, Kevin Short, Daniel Windsor, and especially Eli Garsilazo, for their crafting of the maps, models, and drawings.

During its evolution, the project was reviewed by numerous planners. We are especially grateful to Alan Hoffman for his keen insights on transportation and urban development. We also thank John Chase, Deborah Murphy, Roger Sherman, Woody Tescher, and Richard Weinstein for their helpful suggestions.

Though their contributions were largely unknown to them, we must acknowledge the authors of three key texts, without which the concepts could not have developed: the staff of the ARIJ and their *Atlas of Palestine*; A. B. Zahlan for his role as editor of *The Reconstruction of Palestine: Urban and Rural Development*; and Stefano Bianco, author of *Urban Form in the Arab World*. We also drew ideas and inspiration from the published work of planners Yaakov Garb and Rassem Khamaisi.

We deeply appreciate the organizational, communication, and editorial skills brought to this effort by Mary Vaiana and Christina Pitcher. Without their tireless effort, this volume would never have been possible. We also thank the design team at Ph.D and RAND's Peter Hoffman for producing the book so skillfully and swiftly.

Finally, we would like to thank Guilford Glazer for his vision and his generosity, which brought the project into being and saw it through to completion.

Contents

CHAPTER ONE

Introduction

THIS STUDY EXPLORES OPTIONS for creating an infrastructure for a new Palestinian state. It builds on analyses that RAND conducted between 2002 and 2004 to identify the requirements for a successful Palestinian state. That work, *Building a Successful Palestinian State*,[1] surveyed a broad array of political, economic, social, resource, and environmental challenges that a new Palestinian state would face. It also outlined policy options that Palestinians, Israelis, and the international community could pursue to maximize prospects for the state's success.

The research program for this study encompassed a range of approaches to siting and constructing the backbone of infrastructure that all states need and to integrating a potentially large number of refugees[2] into a Palestinian society already experiencing severe population pressures. Palestine has one of the highest fertility and birth rates in the world. If, in addition to the rapid natural population growth, hundreds of thousands of refugees return to the new state, it would severely stress the already meager ability of a Palestinian government to house, educate, employ, and care for its population. An influx of refugees would also strain social ties in a broader population riven by distinctions between Gazan and West Banker, long-time resident and newcomer, and other more local identities. New migrants will have to overcome divisions among themselves stemming from differences in dialect and habit acquired in their most recent countries of residence.

Our objective was to devise an infrastructure that would, insofar as possible, facilitate solutions to these major challenges. We had no illusion that infrastructure alone would solve them. No single construction project could accomplish that, and, in any case, many of the problems stem from policy choices, social patterns, and collective or individual preferences that are largely unrelated to infrastructure. Nor did we seek to plan precisely how the Palestinian population would be housed, although we estimated the housing requirement. We did not determine how the steadily growing workforce might be employed, although we addressed the demographic and labor market dimension of the problem. Readers seeking analysis of these issues should refer to *Building a Successful Palestinian State*, where they are discussed in detail.

Palestine's Current and Future Demographics

Palestine has a large and rapidly growing population that will strain the ability of the new state to provide basic services and housing over time, even if there were no return of refugees to the new state. As of early 2005, there were approximately 3.6 million people living in the West Bank and Gaza, about 40 percent of the Palestinian population worldwide. This population is growing rapidly: Fertility rates of Palestinian women in the West Bank and Gaza are among the highest in the world, 5.6 and 6.9 children per woman of child-bearing age, respectively. By 2015, the population will be over 5 million. Assuming an influx of perhaps 600,000 returnees, the total population of the West Bank and Gaza could reach nearly 6 million. By 2020, the population in the region could well approach 6.6 million people.

Projections of future population growth depend, among other things, on whether fertility rates in the West Bank and Gaza decline, by how much, and how quickly. There is evidence that the rate is declining, but how quickly is unclear. However, in the short run, births will certainly increase since the number of Palestinian women in the prime childbearing years will more than double. Over the longer term, fertility rates will begin to decline. How much these declines will lower the total fertility rate probably depends on the degree to which the education levels and labor force participation of Palestinian women rise.

Stresses on Palestine's resources are exacerbated by a pronounced youth bulge in the demographic profile: The median age of the population is 16. Thus, demand on key services, especially education and health, will continue to rise, even as the proportion of the population that supports them declines. For example, the ratio of workers to preschool and school-age children in Palestine is 0.73 in the West Bank and 0.60 in

Gaza. In developing countries the ratio is 1.2; in the rest of the Middle East it is 0.96. In developed countries the ratio is 3.1.

The circumstances just described apply to a world in which there has been no large-scale refugee return. If, as anticipated, a final status accord leads to an ingathering of the exiles, the existing situation and the projections based on it will change, perhaps profoundly.

RAND's analysis of migration patterns within the broad diaspora since 1948 suggests that economic factors strongly shaped the trajectory of Palestinian refugees leaving Mandate Palestine, the territory under British control until the creation of Israel, or the Jordanian West Bank in 1967. We expect that economic considerations will also significantly influence the decision of Palestinian refugees to return to Palestine.

Given this assumption, the least likely returnees will be those from countries where incomes are highest and political stability the greatest. The most likely will be those who live in refugee camps in Jordan, Syria, and Lebanon.

How migration will affect overall population growth in Palestine depends crucially on the fertility rate of returning Palestinians and the rate at which they arrive. Refugees from camps in Lebanon, Jordan, and Syria have fertility rates approaching those of Palestinians currently in the West Bank. Taken together, the natural population growth of Palestinians now in the West Bank and Gaza and the influx of refugees and the children they will bear in the coming years will confront the new state with major challenges.

Carrying Capacity

The total capacity of a nation's land and resources to support its population is referred to as "carrying capacity." Palestine's carrying capacity is stretched to the limit. It is one of the most densely populated places in the Arab world at 547 persons per square kilometer. If Gaza is taken separately, it has a population density of 3,457 per square kilometer (9,200 people per square mile), one of the highest in the world.

These figures signify sober realities. Palestinian water consumption is now half the UN minimum daily standard. The physical infrastructure is grossly inadequate, particularly for water, electricity, and sewerage. The demands on Palestine's limited land area for agriculture, infrastructure, economic activity, and housing are growing.[3]

But it is with housing that the problems are most pressing. Currently, there are 6.4 residents on average per housing unit in the West Bank and Gaza, a very large number by developed country standards. If Palestine's population rises from 3.7 million to nearly 6 million over the next ten years, and if current housing densities are to remain stable,

320,000 new housing units will have to be constructed during this period. Simultaneously, a new state would face demands to upgrade or replace a deteriorating physical infrastructure. Solid waste disposal is grossly inadequate, power supply is uneven and sporadic, water supply systems are severely degraded, and the road net is so deteriorated that past investment may be lost.

Economic Pressures

Past rapid rates of population growth have generated a bulge of young people nearing working age. In the coming decade, the number of people reaching working age will be seven times the number of people reaching retirement age. These new labor force entrants will be searching for employment in an economy that has been devastated by the intifada. Opportunities for employment have been few because of the lack of security and the high costs of transportation caused by Israeli curbs on movement of people and goods in the West Bank and Gaza. In addition, job opportunities in Israel, which used to employ 135,000 Palestinians, nearly one-quarter of the Palestinian labor force, have disappeared and are unlikely to return any time soon. As female labor force participation rates rise and these young people enter the labor market, downward pressure on wages and heightening competition for jobs will exacerbate tensions in the current social and political environment. A large influx of refugees of working age, many of whom will be relatively unskilled, would add fuel to the fire.

The Arc: A Formal Structure for a Palestinian State

Palestine's internal formal structure, inadequate for current needs, will soon be called upon to support a much larger population. New concepts for that formal structure are needed, both in its abstract patterns and its concrete infrastructure. RAND's concept for that structure is the Arc.

The Arc is an innovative transportation system along which people and goods will flow throughout the new state. The Arc would link Jenin in the northern West Bank to Gaza City and Gaza Airport through intermediate stops corresponding to Palestine's major cities and towns: Tubas, Nablus, Salfit, Ramallah/Jericho, Jerusalem, Bethlehem and Hebron. The transport system will connect to Gaza by the corridor through Israel that is likely to be negotiated as part of an Israeli-Palestinian final status accord.

The concept of the Arc treats Palestine as an urban space, with specific areas dedicated to livable, high-density residences capable of supporting the projected increase in population even after the repatriation of refugees. The transport corridor would also provide the space for a national aqueduct for water, open park land, telecommunications and electric power lines, and gas and fuel pipelines. Mass transportation stations would not be situated in the historic city centers of the major urban centers. Rather, they would be located 8 to 25 kilometers away. Stations would be connected to the urban centers by express and local bus lines.

This arrangement would have a number of virtues. First, it would leave the historic city centers unencumbered by the congestion of a major rail link as well as vehicular traffic. These centers—and the area alongside the transverse routes to the rail stations—could then develop as sustainable commercial and residential centers. A sinuous national park would weave along and across the Arc, preserving the uninhabited elements of Palestine's natural landscape, especially the views looking east to Jordan from the West Bank ridgeline.

Construction of the Arc would provide jobs. When completed it would ensure labor mobility and a feeling of national cohesion by enabling residents to live in one place and work in another by a short, comfortable commute. Until such time as Israeli and Jordanian airports became available, Palestinians and foreign visitors would be able to travel from the Gaza airport to the northern West Bank in 90 minutes.

In addition to these more mundane benefits, the Arc will be a tangible symbol of Palestinian statehood and progress.

---

[1] The RAND Palestinian State Study Team, *Building a Successful Palestinian State*, Santa Monica, Calif.: The RAND Corporation, MG-146-DCR, 2005.

[2] The United Nations Relief and Works Agency (UNRWA) defines Palestinian "refugees" as persons whose normal place of residence was Palestine between June 1946 and May 1948, who lost both their homes and means of livelihood as a result of the 1948 Arab-Israeli conflict, and who registered with UNRWA; and the descendents of registered refugees (see http://www.un.org/unrwa/refugees/whois.html, as of February 8, 2005). Some people who were eligible did not register officially with UNRWA. Also, Palestinians who were displaced from the West Bank and Gaza in 1967 are considered "displaced persons" rather than refugees. Thus not all Palestinians immigrants to a new Palestinian state would be refugees in the formal sense. However, because the debate is usually framed in terms of refugees, we use this term to refer generally to Palestinian immigrants to a new Palestinian state.

[3] Carrying capacity would be helped by refugee compensation provided by international donors.

Figure 1. Formal Structure of the Palestinian Landscape. The landscape's formal structure is a historic pattern of topography, climate, vegetation, and agriculture in relationship to the man-made environment of roads, terraces, towns, and cities.

Chapter Two

Palestine—The Formal Structure of a New State

The Shape of Palestine

EVERY NATION STATE HAS A SHAPE, which is most immediately recognized by the contours of its international borders. But within those borders there is another shape we might call the nation's formal structure—the pattern of constructed human habitation and human movement, set in relationship to the natural environment. The potential formal structure of a new Palestinian state is the focus of this chapter.

National boundaries are essentially political. Whether their outline is organic or geometric—whether it follows the curves of river valleys, sea coasts, and mountain ridges or traces straight lines across desert and plain—the reality of borders is often more conceptual than physical. Borders are also notoriously impermanent; they can change when one nation expands while another contracts. By comparison, the formal structure of hills, rivers, paths, roads, towns, and cities seems more tangible and stable, because the pattern is tied to those inescapable realities of water, rain, sun, and soil that are necessary for human survival, habitation, and industry.

We take as our working assumption that the national boundaries of a new Palestinian state have already been roughly defined in the political arena. (See Figure 2.) Our focus is on the formal structure—both existing and potential—within those borders.

The national boundaries produce, in the West Bank, a shape similar to a kidney bean, with a pronounced indentation just below the middle where Israeli territory extends eastward to incorporate Jerusalem. At its longest, the West Bank runs around 80 miles north to south. At its widest point, between Qalqilya and the Jordan River, it is 35 miles west to east; at its narrowest, the distance between the Old City of Jerusalem and the Jordan River is only 18 miles. The total land area of the West Bank is around 2,200 square miles. Gaza's land area is around 140 square miles. (See Figure 3.)

What we find within Palestine is an ancient understructure of mountains, valleys, wadis, rivers, cities, towns, villages, terraces, fields, and roads. Over the centuries, other elements have been added, such as newer towns and cities, modern roads, railroads, airports, etc. But much of the underlying ancient pattern persists, even as a long series of superimposed political boundaries have come and gone. The present challenge is to adapt this durable understructure to revised political boundaries, creating a new formal structure that can meet the Palestinians' future social and economic needs. That formal structure does not now exist.

From the perspective of human habitation, Palestinian cities, towns, and refugee camps are overcrowded and undersupplied with the basics of urban infrastructure and dignified human habitation. From the perspective of human movement, the necessary flow of goods and people between farmland and town, between town and city, and between Palestine and the outside world has been reduced to a trickle. From the perspective of the relationship to the natural environment, the situation with regard to the supply of water, disposal of waste, consumption of energy, protection of sensitive land, and access to outdoor recreation can fairly be characterized as dire.

There are currently 3.6 million residents of the West Bank and Gaza. The challenge of providing adequate housing, jobs, transportation, and other infrastructure to support this population is daunting enough. Yet the population is expected to nearly double within the next 15 years, exceeding 6 million people, the result of both internal growth and the return of perhaps as many as 750,000 refugees. (See Figure 4.)

Thus Palestine's internal formal structure, inadequate for current needs, will soon be called upon to support twice as many people. New concepts for that formal structure are needed, both in its abstract patterns and its concrete infrastructure. Winston Churchill wrote, "We shape our cities, and they shape us." The ideas in this chapter are offered as starting points for discussion of the form and structure of the nation that the Palestinians themselves will build and that will in turn shape the future of Palestinian national life.

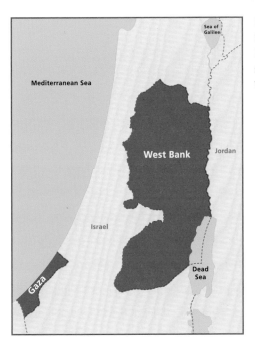

Figure 2. Prospective Shape of a Palestinian State. The project assumes the 1967 "Green Line" as the basis for the ultimate negotiated shape of the Palestinian state, including the West Bank and Gaza.

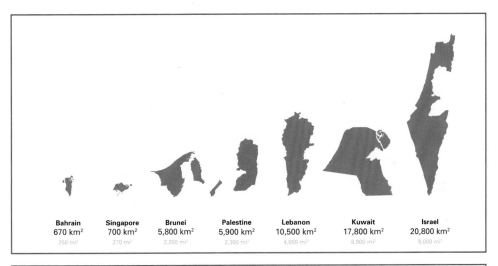

Bahrain	Singapore	Brunei	Palestine	Lebanon	Kuwait	Israel
670 km²	700 km²	5,800 km²	5,900 km²	10,500 km²	17,800 km²	20,800 km²
260 mi²	270 mi²	2,200 mi²	2,300 mi²	4,050 mi²	6,900 mi²	8,000 mi²

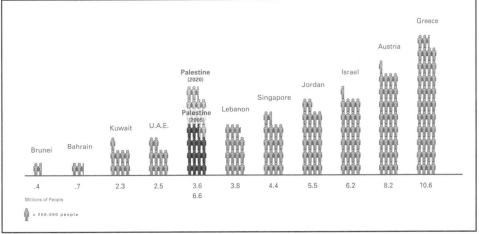

Figure 3 (middle). National Land Areas Compared. The approximate land area of a Palestinian state will likely exceed 2,300 square miles; while small, there are other successful states of this size.

Figure 4 (bottom). National Populations Compared. The current population of the West Bank and Gaza is estimated at 3.6 million people, but it is expected to nearly double within 15 years to more than 6 million.

Density

Problem or Opportunity?

One of the first and most direct ways of describing the physical challenge of a Palestinian state is to measure the number of people relative to the amount of land. With more than 3.6 million people in just over 2,300 square miles, Palestine today has more than 1,400 people per square mile. This population density puts it near the top of the world's densest nations. (See Figure 5.) Europe's densest country, the Netherlands, has 1,200 people per square mile. The world's densest large country, Bangladesh, has 2,200. If Palestine's population increases, as expected, to more than 6 million within the next 15 years, its density will reach 2,400 people per square mile, exceeding even Bangladesh. And this does not even take into account the population density within Gaza, which is currently a staggering 9,200 people per square mile.

High population density is often associated with overcrowding, poverty, disease, traffic congestion, economic anemia, and environmental degradation. As noted, Bangladesh is very densely populated. But so are Singapore and Taiwan, along with the Netherlands. High population density by itself is not necessarily a prescription for national failure.

Indeed, there is something of a reverse correlation when measuring the density of cities as opposed to the density of nations. A growing body of thought and research suggests that in a number of domains—sustainability, environmental performance, reduced energy consumption, livability, even social equity—cities with higher densities may perform better than those with lower densities. Three critical factors associated with these cities are compact urban form, high-density housing, and good public transportation.

According to Kenworthy and Newman in their groundbreaking *Sustainability and Cities: Overcoming Automobile Dependence*, the key to this kind of formal structure is the coupling of higher urban density with a reduced dependence on the car and other private vehicles. Transportation systems themselves strongly reflect and influence the population density of cities and nations. Where automobile-based systems dominate, densities are dramatically lower. For example, many cities in Australia and the United States—such as Houston, Phoenix, Adelaide, and Brisbane—are generally oriented to the automobile and have typical average metropolitan densities of around 3,000 people per square mile (urban density figures are typically much higher than national figures

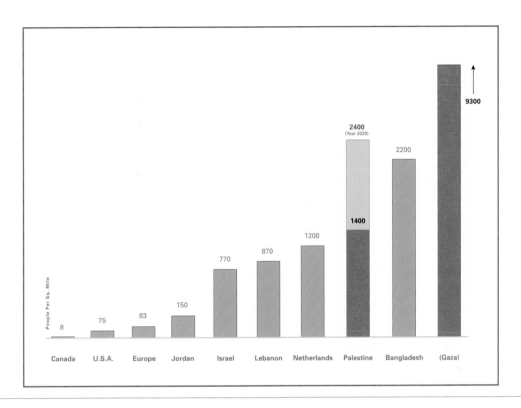

Figure 5. National Population Densities Compared. The current population of the West Bank and Gaza places the current Palestinian territories in the ranks of other high-density countries such as Lebanon and the Netherlands. If population growth projections are accurate, a Palestinian state would surpass even Bangladesh in national density; already, today, Gaza on its own is over four times more densely populated than Bangladesh.

because agricultural and undeveloped land is excluded). In cities with extensive, high-performing public transportation systems combined with effective land use controls, densities tend to be significantly higher. Thriving Asian and European cities such as Singapore, Paris, and Munich have densities at least ten times as high, averaging 30,000 people per square mile across their metropolitan areas. (See Figure 6.)

Thus the current and projected high population density of a Palestinian state, if combined with certain patterns of higher-density urban development and public transportation, could be an asset in the search for a sustainable formal structure for the state.

Cultural, Climactic, and Economic Factors

There are three factors indicating that a compact, higher-density, transit-based formal structure could be appropriate and successful for Palestine in particular. The residential density of cities is rooted in numerous cultural preferences. Cultures vary widely with respect to preferred or acceptable housing types, ranging from freestanding villas or cottages, to attached row houses, to courtyard houses for extended families, to apartments in low-rise or even high-rise elevator buildings. The reasons for such diverse housing preferences are numerous: marital and family traditions, domestic habits, attitudes toward the natural environment, architectural traditions, responses to climate, economic prosperity, defensive considerations, property law, and banking practices. But regardless of the forces that produce them, the specific type or mix of housing types has a profound effect on urban form. In the English-speaking world, the cultural orientation toward the freestanding home has helped foster the conditions for urban sprawl. In Paris, two centuries of middle class adaptation to apartment living has sustained exceptionally high densities, exceeding 80,000 people per square mile within the central city. In Palestine specifically, and throughout the Middle East, there are numerous rich traditions of higher-density habitations, from the traditional "hosh" to a range of courtyard buildings and urban apartment dwellings. Even small, ancient villages frequently exhibit the compactness and higher residential density now associated with sustainable urban form. (See Figure 7.)

While some of these housing forms are rooted in cultural norms and social arrangements of the Middle East, they are also tied to the region's climatic and topographic conditions, which are often severe or even inhospitable. The prevailing influences of the desert, hilly terrain, rocky soil, strong winds, and aridity all have contributed, suggests urban planner John Meunier,[1] to a tradition of compactness that is many thousands of years old. (See Figure 8.) Meunier goes so far as to suggest that in arid climates around

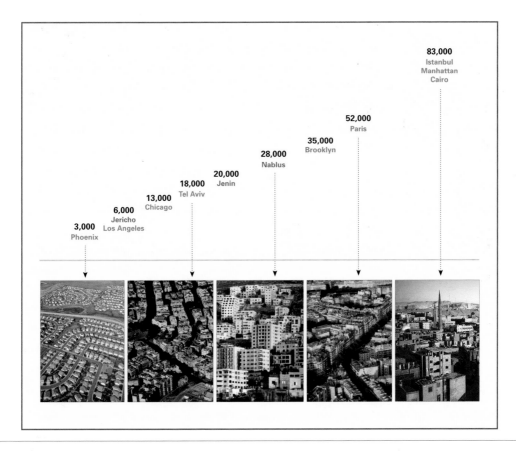

83,000
Istanbul
Manhattan
Cairo

52,000
Paris

35,000
Brooklyn

28,000
Nablus

20,000
Jenin

18,000
Tel Aviv

13,000
Chicago

6,000
Jericho
Los Angeles

3,000
Phoenix

Figure 6. Population Densities Within Urban Areas Compared. Most Palestinian cities fall within the middle range of urban population density, which is considered more favorable for sustainability than the low densities of urban sprawl.

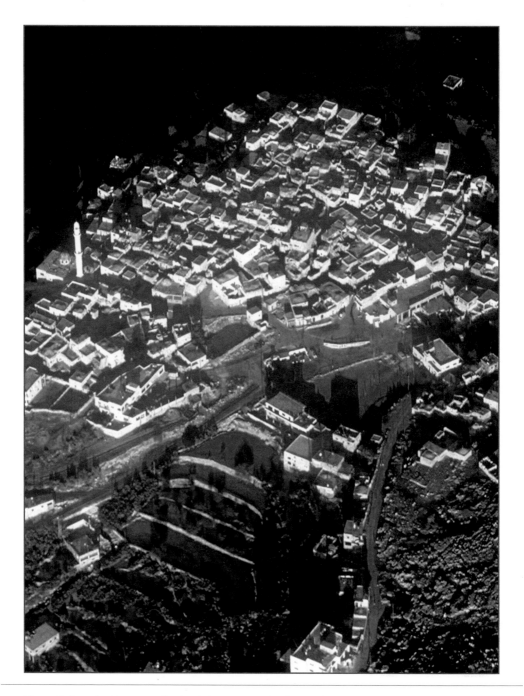

Figure 7. Sustainable Form of Palestinian Towns. The form of the typical town in Palestine is sustainable: high density and compact, walkable, mixed in its uses, and closely fitted to the terrain.

Figure 8. Urban Compactness Preserves Open Space. The principle of compact towns and cities with higher densities preserves open space in the surrounding area for agriculture, recreation, and natural reserves.

the world typical historic urban densities were in the range of 35,000 people per square mile. This is almost identical to the levels of density that researchers now suggest may be optimal in achieving sustainable urban form.

Another factor that can influence both national and urban density is the existence of a national automobile industry. Countries with enormous investments in car manufacturing such as the United States, France, and Japan—and now to a growing extent China—increasingly find themselves in the conflicted position of promoting automobile use to enhance industrial performance, all the while paying the growing social, environmental, and economic price that automobile-generated pollution and sprawl are destined to exact. (Japan has avoided this to a considerable extent because its automobile production is intentionally focused more on exports than on the domestic market.) Palestine does not have and is unlikely to have an automobile industry. From the perspective of creating a sustainable formal structure for the nation, that may turn out to be an advantage. The absence of automobile manufacturing combined with an underdeveloped road system and low levels of vehicle ownership may actually provide Palestinians with an opportunity to "leapfrog" past the planning mistakes of countries that have created their own dependence on the automobile. This is the contention of Yaakov Garb in his paper on sustainable transport.[2] He and other planners in Israel have long identified their country's growing dependence on the car and the resulting urban sprawl as a major problem in both the near and long term. He asks, "Will Palestine follow Israel along the road to mass motorization or will it choose the path of sustainability?" This report is premised on the latter: The new formal structure of Palestine should be sustainable—socially, economically, urbanistically, and environmentally—and public transportation provides the key to sustainability.

Target Density in the West Bank

In planning for an additional Palestinian population of 3 million within 15 years, the first and most obvious step is to propose exempting Gaza from any additional population burden. Its extraordinary density suggests that, to the contrary, efforts should be made to reduce the population there, or at least to provide the existing 1.3 million people with improvements in all aspects of the physical environment, not new neighbors.[3]

Therefore, the question of where and how to help locate 3 million new people should be confined to the West Bank. The West Bank comprises slightly less than 2,200 square miles. Though much larger than Gaza, this is a relatively small area, which immediately begs the question of what the target average density for urban areas should be.

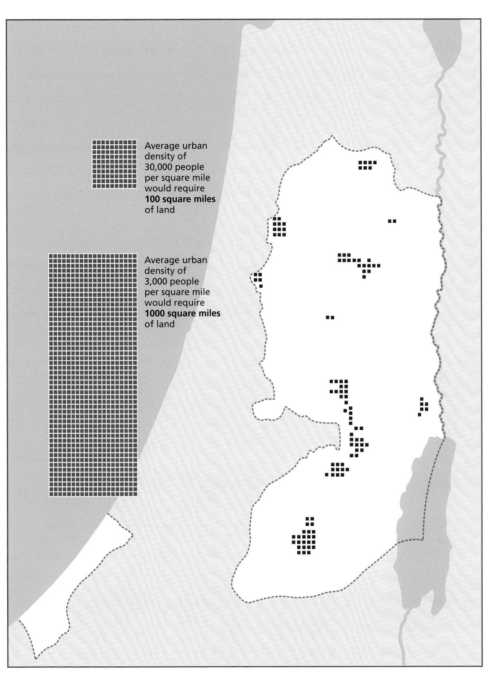

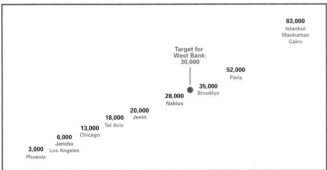

Figure 9 (top). Comparative Land Area Required for Low-Density Versus High-Density Growth.
For 3 million additional people, new development at an average 3,000 people per square mile
would require 1,000 square miles of land. If the density is increased to 30,000 people per square
mile, only 100 square miles are required.

Figure 10 (bottom). Target Density for West Bank Cities. The Arc assumes a target average density for West Bank cities of 30,000 people per square mile within built-up areas.

As indicated earlier, low density auto-oriented sprawl typically yields average densities of about 3,000 people per square mile—with its comparably arid setting, Phoenix, Arizona, is a relevant example. For the projected new Palestinian population, such low density would require a "footprint" of 1,000 square miles, that is, nearly half of the entire West Bank. (See Figure 9.) There would be little buildable land left. In other words, even if Palestinians were to overlook the disadvantages of sprawl and choose or allow such a pattern to emerge, the resulting land coverage would constitute an environmental disaster. Because of its relatively small size, the West Bank cannot afford the spatial "luxury" of sprawl.

We recommend instead setting a target average density in urbanized areas of 30,000 people per square mile. (See Figure 10.) This density is well suited to cities with sustainable design, transit-oriented urban development, and compactness appropriate to arid regions. Indeed, similar densities already can be found today in parts of Bethlehem, Hebron, Jerusalem, and Nablus. With such densities as a given, the required overall footprint within the West Bank would be dramatically reduced by a factor of ten—to 100 square miles.

Existing Pattern of Towns and Linkages in the West Bank

If 100 square miles is needed for urban development at the target density, where and how could this development be distributed most effectively in the West Bank? Trying to answer such a question requires an assessment of the existing structure of West Bank cities and towns and the linkages between them.

A first striking feature of Palestinian villages, towns, and cities is that they are not evenly distributed across the West Bank but are grouped almost entirely in its western half. Clearly this is a historic and enduring response to topography and climate. The region is cut in half from north to south by a slightly curving line, or arc, of mountain ridges. (See Figure 11.) In some areas, the ridgeline reaches more than 3,000 feet above sea level, with more typical heights ranging between 2,000 and 2,500 feet. Because of the prevailing winds from west to east off the Mediterranean Sea, the West Bank experiences the storm pattern typical of "West Coast Mediterranean" climate zones (from California to South Africa), whereby the rising elevation of the mountains causes most

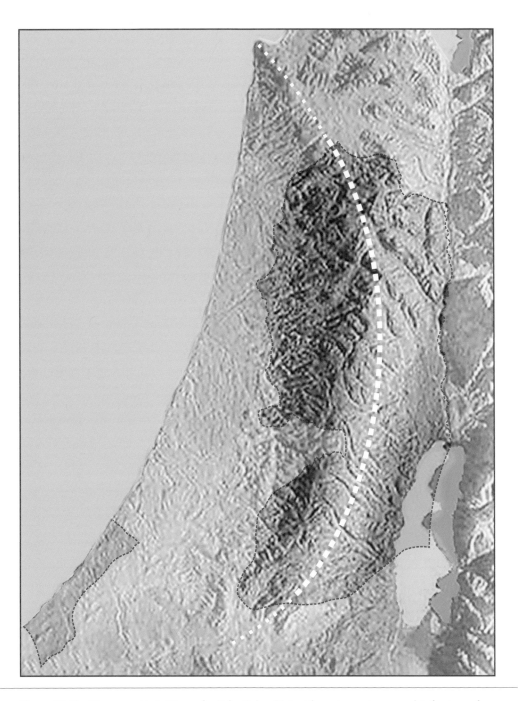

Figure 11. The Topographic Setting of a Palestinian State. The primary topographic feature of the West Bank is the slightly curving north-south line, or arc, of mountain ridges.

rain to drop on the westerly face of the ridgeline, leaving the eastern face relatively dry. The ridgeline also puts the eastern slopes in a "wind shadow," making them not only dryer but also hotter. The result is what the *Atlas of Palestine*[4] identifies as sharply different agro-ecological zones on either side of the ridgeline: the "Central Highlands" to the west, the "Eastern Slopes" to the east (additionally, there is a small third zone designated "Semi-Coastal" in the West Bank's northwest corner, plus a narrow fourth zone along the Jordan River). The sharp break of zones along the arc of ridges helps explains why Palestinian habitation has remained generally in the west of the West Bank, with its significantly higher rainfall,[5] arable land, and occasional cooling breezes. (See Figure 12.) The notable exception to this pattern is the low-lying oasis of Jericho, whose plentiful and accessible underground water supply has sustained an ancient town in an otherwise inhospitably hot and arid territory.

Most of the West Bank is hilly, and much of it is steep. The cities, towns, and villages of the West Bank are typically located in the bottom of a valley or wadi (where there would be a source of water, at least seasonally) or rising up the hillsides. A smaller number have been built on hilltops, but usually on more accessible, lower, less steep slopes.

The *Atlas of Palestine* identifies a family of 11 principal cities in the West Bank. They are, from north to south: Jenin, Tubas, Tulkarm, Nablus, Qalqilya, Salfit, Ramallah, Jericho, Jerusalem, Bethlehem, and Hebron[6] (See Figure 13.)

With the exceptions of Tulkarm and Qalqilya in the west and Jericho in the east, they are loosely arrayed along or near the path of the ridgeline arc. The three largest in population are Jerusalem (250,000), Hebron (154,000), and Nablus (127,000). The next two largest—Tulkarm and Qalqilya—are considerably smaller, with just over 40,000 each.

The geographic area spanned by the primary West Bank cities is relatively small—more akin to a single, integrated metropolitan region than a dispersed national constellation of cities. To illustrate this regional scale, we compare the West Bank cities with a number of other urban clusters. (See Figure 14.) Metropolitan Cairo is a region with a dominant "mother city," are linked to a similar linear array of smaller cities and towns. The linear arrangement derives from the influence of geography: The attraction of either a fertile river valley. The San Francisco Bay region is also organized in a north-south line because of the elongated bay, but with the significant difference that there are several primary (i.e., large and economically independent) cities—Oakland, San Jose, and San Francisco. This clustering of independent cities within a single metropolitan region also defines the main urban complex of the Netherlands, known as the Randstad. This

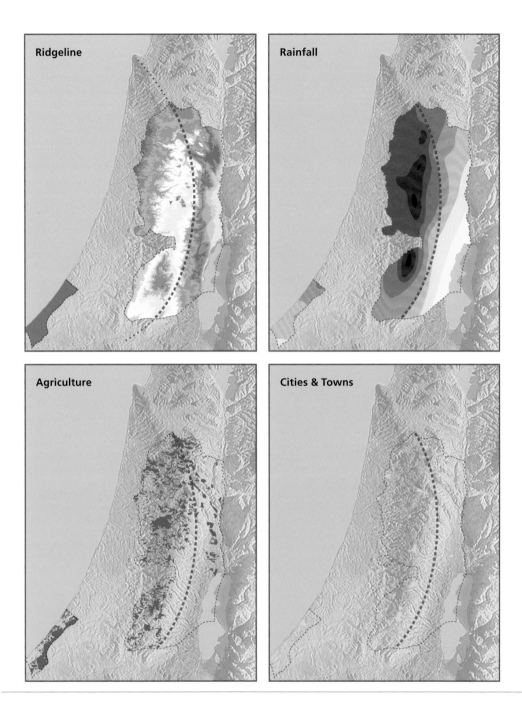

Figure 12. A Natural Arc Reflected in the Manmade Landscape.
The Atlas of Palestine shows that an arc of mountain ridges
divides the Mediterranean ecosystem to the west from the arid
slopes on the east. Because rainfall is significantly higher on the
western side, agriculture is concentrated there, along with the
great majority of historic Palestinian cities, towns, and villages.

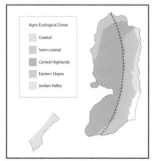

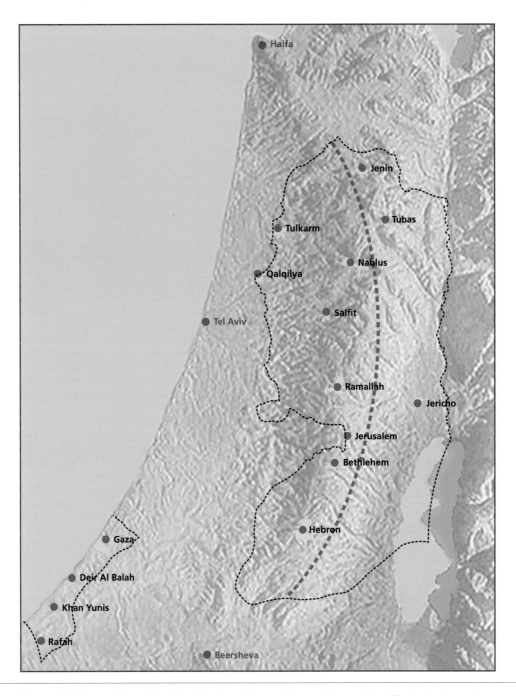

Figure 13. Primary Cities of the West Bank and Gaza. Fifteen cities are identified as "primary"; four are in Gaza, eleven in the West Bank.

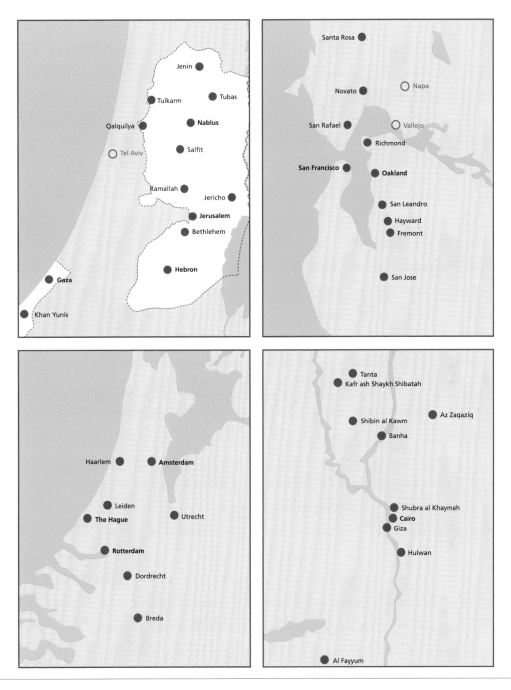

Figure 14. Scale of West Bank Compared to Other Metropolitan Regions. The geographic area spanned by the primary West Bank cities is relatively small—akin to a single, integrated metropolitan region. The comparative examples include those with a single dominant city (Cairo), and multiple primary cities (the Randstad area in the Netherlands and the San Francisco Bay area).

0 5 10   20 mi

integrated region includes four major cities—Amsterdam, the Hague, Rotterdam, and Utrecht—and several secondary ones such as Delft, Haarlem, and Leiden. This example offers a useful model of a decentralized but integrated urban region on a scale similar to the territory of the West Bank.

Many of the West Bank cities have been settled for millennia—notably Hebron, Bethlehem, Jerusalem, Jericho, and Nablus—and it is not surprising that there are ancient roadways that connect them, as the region has always been a crossroads for trade. Indeed, the current path of Route 60, the north-south highway of the West Bank, follows quite closely the ancient route that linked these cities. Route 60 today is for the most part relatively narrow, winding, and slow. This reflects two conditions. The first is the lack of investment in upgrading the West Bank's infrastructure. The second is that on a regional basis, north-south traffic often preferred the flatter coastal routes between, say, Cairo and Damascus. A 1948 map of the remains of the Turkish and British Railway system underscores the fact that investment in the West Bank has tended to focus on east-west links rather than on north-south ones. Today, it becomes clear that within the borders of a new Palestinian state, the lack of a faster north-south internal link will inhibit the efficient movement of goods and people necessary for economic growth. (See Figure 15.)

The discussion of existing conditions cannot conclude without addressing the numerous Israeli settlements in the West Bank and the roads built to serve them. These constitute an almost autonomous urban system. Many of the settlements break the traditional barrier west of the arc. Most are situated on hilltops, ignoring long established practice in the region. They depend for their existence on expensive infrastructure and technology—roads, automobiles, air conditioning, pumped water supply, and mechanical irrigation. They are largely isolated from built-up urban areas and from their immediate surroundings. As a result, they are dependent for transport primarily on private vehicles rather than public transit. For these reasons, we have chosen for the purposes of this study to set the question of Israeli settlements aside. They will certainly be part of the ultimate urban framework in the West Bank, but we believe that solutions for the West Bank need to derive from the primordial pattern of Palestinian habitation. The ultimate disposition of the Israeli settlements should follow, not lead, the analysis.

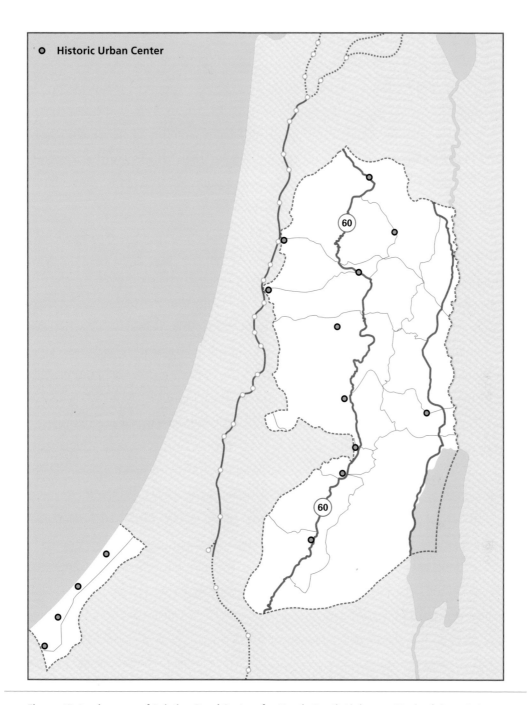

Figure 15. Inadequacy of Existing Road System for North-South Linkages. Much of the existing West Bank road system has been focused, historically and in the present, on east-west linkages between the mountains and the coastline. There is only one continuous north-south road— Route 60—linking the cities arrayed along the arc of the mountain ridgeline. It is inadequate for the necessary connections and infrastructure of an independent Palestinian state. The Trans-Israel Highway is shown in gray for comparison.

Models of Distribution

Given the location, size, and linkages of existing Palestinian towns and cities, we can return to the question of how a 100-square-mile footprint for new habitation might be distributed within the boundaries of the West Bank. There are many different models of urban distribution within a region; the study team chose to focus on four distinct models for consideration. (See Figures 16a and 16b.)

"Hub" Model (Single Mega-City)

In this model, a single large new city accommodates at least three million people. The city would exist either in relative isolation or in proximity to an existing city (most likely in the Jerusalem/Jericho region). This approach falls in the tradition of new national or provincial capital cities such as Brasilia, Canberra, Chandigarh, and Washington. It should be distinguished from a "new towns" strategy in which freestanding satellite settlements are developed on the periphery of an existing city.

The history of new capitals suggests that they require decades if not centuries to take shape and become successful urban areas. Because the creation of new cities is often driven by ideological or political purposes rather than economic or commercial needs, they may struggle with an inherent economic lethargy.

The creation of a new city has the potential advantages of centralized development and administrative control. Its situation in an open landscape presents opportunities to create strong and positive symbols for the nation. But the disadvantages of this approach are significant. The focus of resources on one city may create a "boom" effect, with explosive population growth and land speculation. It may monopolize public funding and focus to the detriment of all other urbanized areas. Even if these disadvantages could be overcome, the team believes that sufficient contiguous, buildable, and suitable land is most likely not available in the West Bank. Furthermore, a mega-city would require an expensive, centralizing infrastructure of roads, water, and electricity. Such a network does not exist, and the cost of building the new city could well deplete funds for construction of the needed interurban linkages. The most pessimistic scenario is an overcrowded, unsustainable urban center poorly linked to the rest of the nation.

"Tripod" Model (Three Large Cities)

An alternative approach would be to guide urban development to the three largest exist-

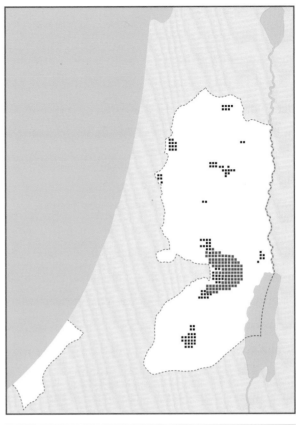

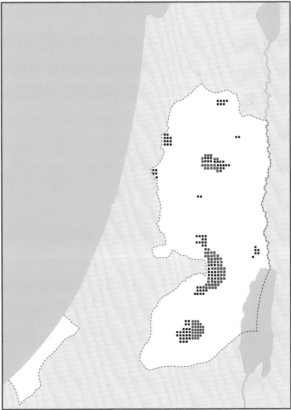

■ New Urban Area
■ Existing Urban Area

Figure 16a. Four Possible Population Distribution Models. The advantages and disadvantages of four different population distribution models were assessed. The first two were eliminated because of the lack of needed land and risk of overcrowding.

ing cities: Jerusalem, Hebron, and Nablus. There is a certain logic to distributing the costs and burdens of growth to the three largest cities rather than to a single new center. But the team remains concerned that even dividing a new population of three million people to three areas may result in cities that are overly crowded and unable to support the demand. The team is also concerned that even in this scenario, insufficient land would be available to meet the need. Finally, the focus on three cities may leave other important cities overlooked and poorly connected to a national infrastructure framework.

"Net" Model (Scattered Towns and Cities)

Distributing new growth more or less evenly all across the West Bank is attractive in concept because it spreads the burdens and benefits of growth equally. Almost all towns and cities could enjoy some economic benefit, and this approach could encourage greater local control. But scattered development probably requires the most miles of infrastructure at the highest cost. Indeed, so much connective infrastructure would be required that setting project priorities would be a constant and vexing problem for any national administration. Such distributed growth may itself encourage political "balkanization," undermining larger regional and national institutions and initiatives.

"Linear" Model (Chain of Many Cities)

The relatively elongated shape of the West Bank and the linear organizing effect of the topographic arc suggest a fourth approach of connecting most of the major cities along a single trunk line. This could potentially connect more of the West Bank population at the least cost. The chain of cities could provide focus and direction for new economic development while helping to revitalize the principal existing historic centers. By encouraging each urban area to grow in a linear—or "branch"—form to link to the national trunk line, compact and sustainable urban form is favored over undirected and unbounded growth. The approach relates growth to existing topographic and habitation patterns, with the potential to create a strong national symbol through the connective infrastructure itself, rather than exclusively through expensive and possibly wasteful individual architectural monuments. The disadvantages of this approach are that it may favor central areas of the West Bank at the expense of the eastern and western zones, and that if incorrectly implemented, it may create too much urban development along the line of the arc itself.

On the basis of this analysis, the team selected the linear model as having the most promise for further investigation.

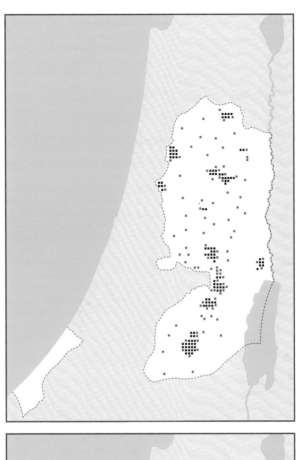

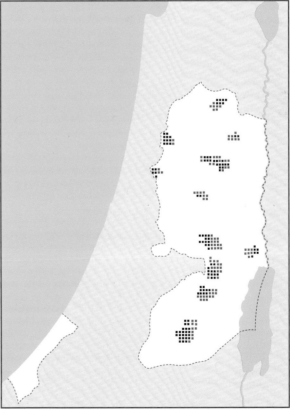

■ New Urban Area
■ Existing Urban Area

Figure 16b. Four Possible Population Distribution Models. The third model distributed benefits widely but had the highest cost with respect to linking infrastructure. The fourth had the widest distribution of benefit and greatest regional integration at the least cost for linking infrastructure, while corresponding most closely to the natural arc in the landscape.

Linking the Cities: The Need for an Alternate to Route 60

The linear model puts an emphasis on the existing chain of cities along the central spine of the West Bank. Population growth and urban development would be directed to this line. The immediate question raised is how the cities would be linked to each other.

The historic centers of most of the cities are already linked by the roadway called Route 60. This route, however, is inadequate for the future needs of the state. Traffic on the road is necessarily slowed as each metropolitan area is approached and entered. For those traveling longer distances, the route itself may disappear on one side of the city, only to reappear on the other.

One option for national development would be to improve Route 60, by widening and permitting greater speed and by creating bypass roads around major cities. However, this strategy runs the risk of encouraging greater development along Route 60 while increasing traffic and congestion. The existing development along much of the route would make it difficult to add a separate public transportation right-of-way. If improperly expanded, Route 60 has the potential to induce a crippling combination of growth and congestion along its corridor. Route 60 should be upgraded, but an alternate faster route should also be developed.

National Infrastructure: The Arc

The need for a north-south link and the presence of the north-south arc in the topographic landscape create the intriguing prospect of a major new project parallel to the path of the arc. The primary function of such a project would be to provide the major transportation link for the West Bank. Its path and length—a 70-mile curve from Hebron to Jenin—arguably would connect the highest number of existing built-up areas in the shortest distance and at the least cost.[7] The construction of the transportation line would invite the concurrent parallel construction of other needed lines for electricity, natural gas, telecommunications, and water. A national linear park could weave back and forth across the line as influenced by the landscape. The ensemble could have great symbolic power for the new nation. We propose to call it simply the Arc. (See Figures 17 and 18.)

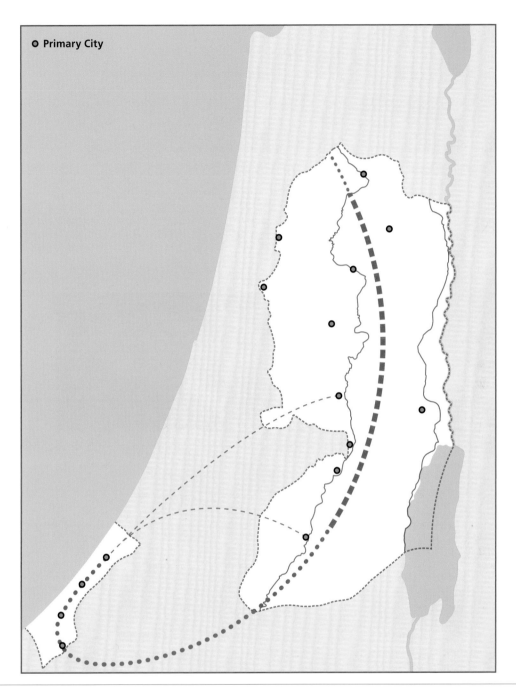

○ **Primary City**

Figure 17. The Arc—A Corridor for National Integration and Infrastructure. The Arc is a proposed national corridor of varying width that would integrate and connect the cities of the West Bank to each other, and all of the West Bank to Gaza. This corridor is in effect a third link between Gaza and the West Bank, in addition to the two "safe passage" routes that have been envisioned in previous diplomatic accords.

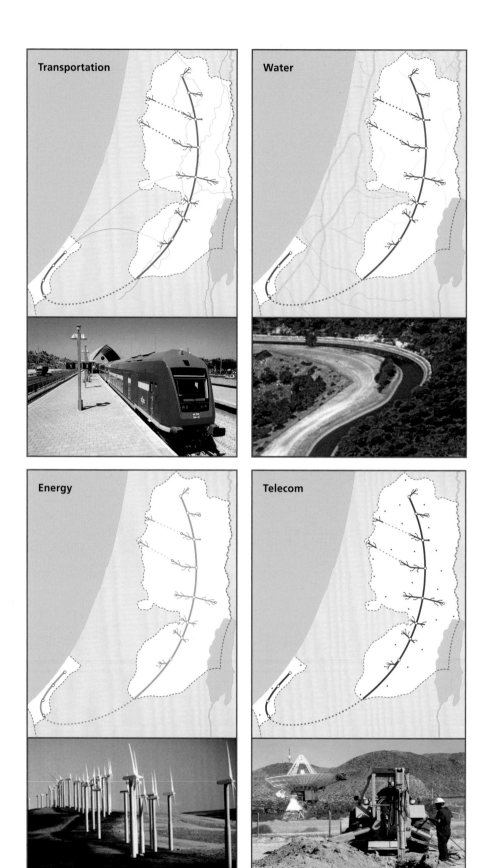

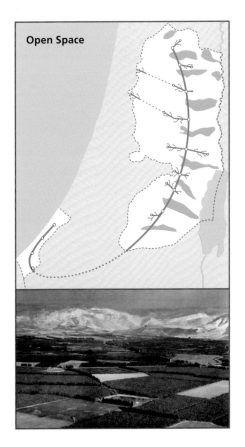

Open Space

Figure 18. The Arc—Five Infrastructures. The Arc is the proposed trunk line of the Palestinian national infrastructure corridor, linking Gaza and the West Bank. It includes a rapid rail line, a national water carrier, energy generation and transmission, telecommunications lines, and a national linear park. Each of the infrastructures has east-west lateral branches that create the framework for linear development in each urban area and the boundaries for the national open space system of parks, forests, reserves, and farmlands.

Figure 19. Precedents for National Infrastructure. Transformative infrastructure projects have a long history, from the ancient aqueducts of Rome to modern water carriers and high speed train networks. These projects typically provide important logistical transport of people, goods, and resources, while also transforming the psychological landscape of the nation-state. In their visible physical manifestations, they also frequently serve as powerful symbols of national enterprise.

Though concrete in its ultimate realization, the Arc is initially conceived as a territorial zone of varying width—perhaps ranging from several hundred feet to a half mile wide, depending on the local circumstances—which can accommodate many types of national infrastructure.

Large-scale infrastructure projects that transform the psychological and physical landscape of nations have a long history, from the ancient Roman aqueducts and the modern water carriers of the American West and Israel to the growing network of high-speed trains in Japan and Europe. (See Figure 19.)

The long-term effects of such infrastructure projects have often proved significant, if not decisive, for their respective national economies. In the shorter term, such initiatives function as public works projects that create jobs and generate considerable associated economic activity. In the case of the Arc, numerous scenarios are conceivable: beginning construction at one end and proceeding to the other; beginning at the middle and working outwards in two directions; or beginning at numerous points along the line, with an eventual fusion of all segments. Decisions about such phasing and sequencing can take into account a variety of economic, social, and political factors. These scenarios can provide Palestinian leaders with a range of options on where and when to direct construction and development activity. In any scenario, the nature of the project is estimated to create a significant number of jobs (see the chapter on cost estimates and economic benefits), ranging from manual labor and transport to surveying and engineering. (See Figure 20.)

From a logistical perspective, the creation of a single linear zone of construction for multiple uses, while requiring a high degree of coordination, can save on construction costs and reduce the extent of disruption from construction. Once a trench has been dug, for example, to make way for concrete footings for a rail line or roadway, the same trench can be used to locate conduit or pipes for telecommunications (such as fiber-optic cable), water supply, natural gas, storm water removal, sanitary sewage removal, and so forth. (See Figure 21.) If a national aqueduct is incorporated, the visual amenity of flowing water can be made widely accessible through the co-location of the continuous linear park. The generation of electric power from preferred renewable energy sources such as the sun or wind—both plausible options given the climate and ridgeline location—can find expression in photovoltaic installations or windmills. (See Figure 22.) These can visually reinforce the presence of the arc as a concrete symbolic expression of national identity and aspiration, while demonstrating the interrelationship of the natural environment, the land, and human settlement.

Figure 20. The Arc as a Generator of Jobs and Economic Activity. The Arc is conceived not only as long-term linking infrastructure, but as a short- and mid-term generator of local employment and economic activity. Numerous phasing scenarios are possible, giving the Palestinian leadership latitude in determining where and in what order to direct the economic stimulation. A range of jobs from manual labor to support services to engineering would be created.

Figure 21 (left). Efficiency of Building Infrastructure in Parallel. The creation of a single linear zone of construction along the Arc for multiple uses can save on construction costs and reduce the extent of disruption from construction.

Figure 22 (right). Elements of Sustainable Design. The generation of electric power from renewable energy sources such as the sun or wind can find expression in photovoltaic installations or windmills. When renewable energy is combined with compact urban growth, reuse of historic structures, provision of advanced public transportation, preservation of open space, and environmental regulation, the fundamentals of sustainable national development are in place.

Interurban Rail

The primary objective of the Arc would be to provide frequent, reliable and high-speed rail service between the primary cities of the West Bank and ultimately—via a 70-mile extension—to the international airport and cities in Gaza. (See Figures 23a and 23b.)

This central emphasis on public transportation derives not only from the critical need for national linkages but also from the correlation between sustainability, urban form, and public transport. It is the premise of the Arc concept that in creating a new Palestinian state, the Palestinians have the opportunity to avoid an unsustainable over-dependence on the private automobile and its physical counterpart, urban sprawl. While automobiles and roadways will be a necessary part of the national infrastructure (see Roadways section below), the interurban rail line of the Arc is the defining and essential investment in realizing a vision of a sustainable, livable national landscape. (See Figure 24.)

The precise nature of the rail service would require careful study. But comparisons may be helpful. Commuter rail service of comparable size can be found, for example, in the San Francisco Bay area. Israel has a 350-mile network that is a primarily north-south system linking Beersheba in the south to Haifa in the north. (See Figure 25.)

The total length of the Arc from Jenin south to Hebron would be approximately 70 miles. The extension south to Gaza would add another 70 miles, bringing the total to 140. At some future time, a northward extension to Haifa city and port could add another 40 miles.

The selection of the type of rail service and vehicle technology would require careful study. On a preliminary basis, however, we suggest that a "light rail" or trolley system is probably not fast enough or capable of carrying adequate loads over the long term; on the other hand, very high-speed rail (such as the TGV system in France) may be unnecessary given the relatively short distance to be covered and close spacing of the stations.

At first glance, it may be tempting to think of the Arc as providing the kind of "commuter rail" service found in many metropolitan areas from San Francisco to Paris to Tokyo. And indeed it should be possible for workers to use the rail service to commute from home to work. But a crucial distinction to be made is that most commuter rail systems are organized on a "hub-and-spoke" model around a single, dominant metropolitan center. Since the conception of the Arc is more of an archipelago of medium-sized cities, a more fruitful analogy may be the unusually closely spaced cities along the Rhine in Germany's Westphalia region—Arnhem (Netherlands), Duisberg, Dusseldorf, Cologne, Bonn, and Koblenz. Linked by national (and international) rail service, the stations for these medium-sized cities are only 10 to 30 minutes apart. They

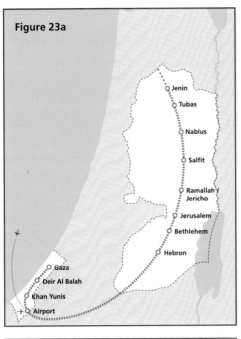

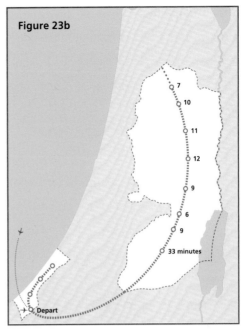

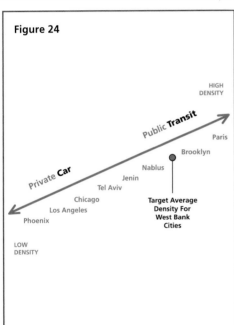

Figures 23a and 23b. The Interurban Rail Line. The critical infrastructure along the Arc is a fast interurban rail line linking almost all the primary cities of Gaza and the West Bank in just over 90 minutes. The rail line makes public transportation a national priority while establishing the "trunk" of the national infrastructure corridor.

Figure 24. Sustainable Transport. The Arc concept is based on the premise that the long-term sustainability and livability of the Palestinian landscape and cities depend on the provision of high-quality public transportation and the discouragement of mass motorization.

Figure 25. Comparison of Israeli Rail System with the Arc. The Israeli national rail system, including intercity and commuter rail, provides a useful comparison for a north-south system on a similar scale.

form a north-south chain of independent cities that, despite their proximity, remain separate and identifiable. Significantly, they have not merged into a continuous "conurbation"; there remains open space, agriculture, and small towns between the built-up urban areas. The maintenance of such open space between existing cities is a key feature of the Arc concept.

National Linear Park

Aside from the practical and functional infrastructure of the Arc, it offers the promise of a great national park or nature preserve that safeguards the land and links the country together. (See Figure 26.) The particular character and uses would require careful study, but conceptually, it ought to be possible to take a brief walk or bike ride along the linear park within the metropolitan area of, say, Nablus or Bethlehem; or, more ambitiously, to undertake a hike or ride along the full extent of the Arc. Elements could include promenades with viewing terraces; hiking, horse, and bike trails; oasis gardens and olive groves; environmental awareness stations and programs; tours of solar and wind power installations; and visual connections, observation decks, and tours related to the aqueduct and its infrastructure. Because of the steep falloff to the Jordan Valley and the Dead Sea, many points along the eastern slopes should offer exceptional vista points of the river, the sea, and the mountains of Jordan; these vista points could become integral to the national linear park.

National Open Space System (Between the Cities)

The national open space system could be developed by merging two existing environmental systems: the extensive landscape of agricultural fields, terraces, groves, and the farms and villages associated with them and the collection of protected forests and nature preserves already designated throughout the West Bank. These two systems can be joined and linked by the national linear park running along the Arc. (See Figure 27.) The system can be supplemented with active and passive recreational opportunities in the mountains and the wadis; protection of ecologically important zones; designation of protected green "fingers" of open space between the branches of the bounded metropolitan areas; enhancement of scenic or historic landscapes and vistas; and protection and upgrading of rural sites of archeological, historic, or religious significance. The open space system would be a reflection of the national policy of establishing clear boundaries of urban growth and of protecting agricultural land from suburbanization and urban sprawl. (See Figure 28.)

Figure 26. National Linear Park. The Arc itself offers the opportunity to interweave built infrastructure and open space with a national linear park. The park would offer numerous opportunities for recreation within each municipal area, as well as paths and facilities for hiking or bicycling between urban areas. The park would also serve as a symbol of national commitment to sustainable urban development and stewardship of the land.

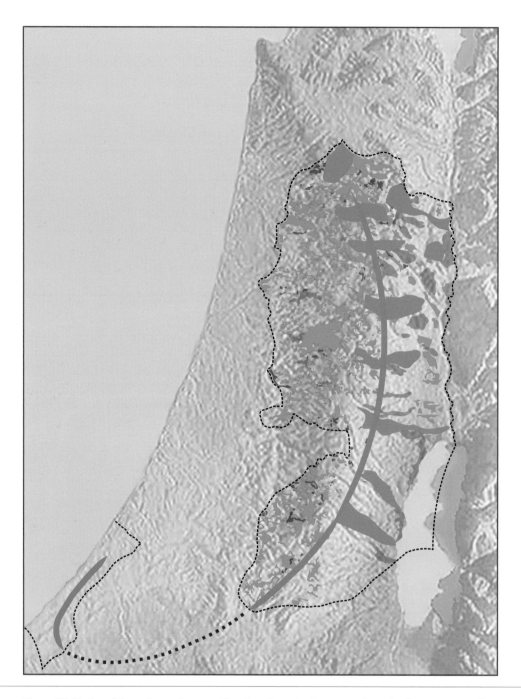

Figure 27. National Open Space System. The directing of urban growth to the linear metropolitan frameworks along the Arc relieves pressure for development on the open space systems of agriculture, forests, nature reserves, and other undeveloped land. This clear distinction between the built and unbuilt environments is contingent on the provision of excellent public transportation and the discouragement of auto-related urban sprawl.

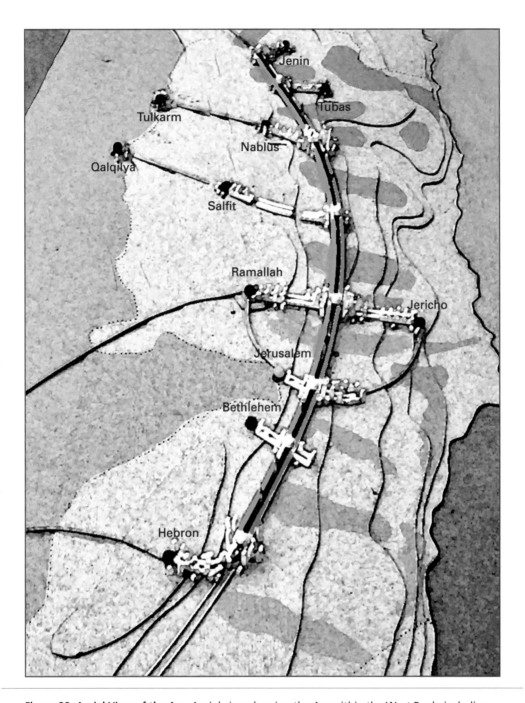

Figure 28. Aerial View of the Arc. Aerial view showing the Arc within the West Bank, including the infrastructure trunk lines, the lateral boulevards or "branches" between the new station areas (white dots) and historic centers (black dots), and the parks and reserves of the national open space system.

Municipal Infrastructure: The Branches

While the Arc and its stations form the trunk of the national infrastructure, they are intended to help shape and stimulate urban growth—or branches—within each municipality. The formal concept of the Arc is to produce—at each city—two poles and a link between them. One pole is the new station area; the other pole is the historic core of the city. Between them is a new boulevard system with integrated rapid transit (See Figure 29.) In this way, three distinct zones for urban development and expansion are created: the historic center, the flanks of the new boulevard, and the area surrounding the station.

Station Area

Conventional practice would locate each new station along the Arc in the historic center of each existing city. However, the Arc concept intentionally sets each station area at a considerable distance—anywhere from 2 to 15 miles—from the historic center. This is done for a number of reasons. First, since there is virtually no existing rail infrastructure in the Palestinian towns and cities, the costs and disruption from intruding the rights-of-way and infrastructure needed for intercity rail would be unacceptably high. Second, the presence of the station in the middle of the existing center would encourage greater concentrations and crowding in settings that are already fairly well built up; the pressure to destroy historic buildings and precincts in order to build denser and higher would only grow with time. Third, a station in the historic center would create pressure for radial growth around the center, creating ever greater problems of access from periphery to center as the city enlarges. By contrast, the proposed remote location of the station encourages a regulated, linear form of expansion from the historic center along a new artery equipped with public transit designed to meet the demands of long-term growth.

Though the station itself would be part of the national infrastructure, the decision about station location should be primarily a local one. Indeed the zone between the station and the historic core should be thought of as municipal infrastructure and, therefore, subject to local planning and control. Palestine has a system of regional authorities called districts or governates. Almost all the cities on the Arc are the designated seats of these regional governments; as such, any administrative or legislative buildings associated with the regional authority would be well located within the station areas, as this would conveniently link all of the authorities together on a national level. (See Figure 30.)

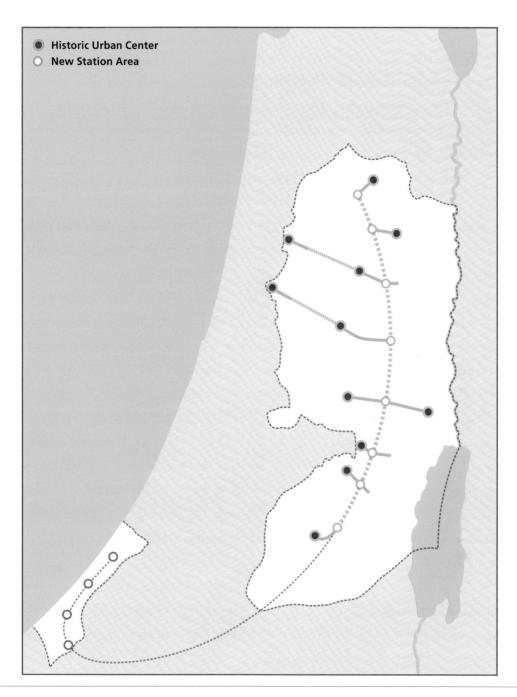

Figure 29. Linking the Station Areas to the Historic Centers. The strategy of locating the new station area at a distance from the historic core is predicated on the construction of a new connective boulevard system between them, typically from 5 to 15 kilometers in length. The boulevard may be a single roadway or a hierarchical system of parallel paths of different size and function. The boulevard structure organizes the growth from the historic core toward the station; it would be configured to accommodate public transit along its length.

The precise ultimate location of each station area along the Arc would be a critical decision for each city because it determines the location of the growth line from the station to the historic city center. The station location will need to be determined based on a number of strategic factors: topography, distance from the existing center, the availability of sufficient buildable terrain and property, the legal disposition of parcels and buildings, the presence of historic or archeological sites, etc.

Wherever the station ends up, it should become attractive for urban development because of its convenience to high-quality interurban rail service. Ideally, all of the station areas along the line should prove similarly attractive because they are relatively close and conveniently linked by train. A perennial problem for developing countries in particular is the tendency toward excessive centralization—for one urban area to become a mega-city that drains investment and economic growth from all other urban centers. One of the goals of the Arc concept is to minimize the differences between the various cities in order to encourage investment and growth more equitably along the line of the Arc and therefore throughout the West Bank.

The stations themselves should be of very high architectural quality, because they will effectively function as the national gateway into each municipal area. The investment in uplifting architectural design not only reinforces an evolving sense of national identity and pride, but such a design is a benefit that can be used and enjoyed by virtually all members of society. In this respect, it would reinforce a commitment to democratic governance discussed in the first volume of this study.[8] The design of such structures also provides an opportunity for architects from Palestine and the region to help define an appropriate architectural language for the new nation. (See Figure 31.)

The station areas should have the potential to attract both public and private investment. (See Figure 32.) They are natural locations for national and international businesses, for larger institutional uses, and for high-density mixed-use neighborhoods. It is hoped that national and international investors would find good reason to construct office buildings, research centers, and wholesale and retail distribution centers around the station areas; while nonprofit sectors would see advantages for the construction there of colleges and universities, hospitals, clinics, and cultural institutions that are inappropriate for the historic core or cannot be accommodated there. (See Figure 33.)

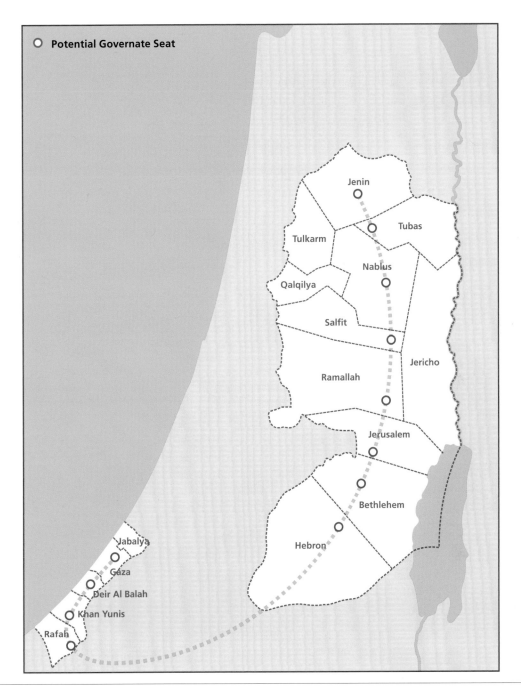

Figure 30. Integrating Regional Governates. The organization of the Arc is intended to promote local and regional oversight of urban development within each governate while fostering national political and administrative coherence. Each station area is thus presented as an appropriate strategic location for the administrative seat of each governate; most of the seats would then be collectively linked by the transport infrastructure of the Arc.

Figure 31. Transport Infrastructure as a Source of National Identity and Pride. The stations themselves should be of very high architectural quality, because they will effectively function as the national gateways into each municipal area. The investment in uplifting architectural design not only reinforces an evolving sense of national identity and pride, but provides a benefit that can be used and enjoyed by virtually all members of society.

Figure 32. Investment at Station Areas. The station areas should both attract both public uses and private investment from national and international businesses. This could include office buildings, research centers, and wholesale and retail distribution centers, all of which would be within convenient distance of the national interurban rail line and toll road along the Arc. Well-integrated new neighborhoods with a mix of uses would also be encouraged.

Figure 33. Station Areas as Sites for Large Civic Institutions. The station areas should also provide convenient sites for larger institutions such as colleges and universities, hospitals, clinics, and cultural centers that are inappropriate for the historic core or cannot be accommodated there. Such institutions would enjoy access on a national scale because of their proximity to the intercity rail service and roadway along the Arc.

Transit Boulevard

The strategy of locating the new station area at a distance from the historic core is predicated on the construction of a new connective boulevard system between them. The boulevard may be a single roadway or a hierarchical system of parallel paths of different sizes and functions. The boulevard structure organizes the growth from the historic core toward the station, since in the short term the core is likely to swell, even overcrowd, as the first wave of refugees returns. Pressure to expand can be directed along the sides of the boulevard, where new neighborhoods can be developed.

The boulevard itself should be configured to accommodate public transit along its length. The emerging form of transit known as Bus Rapid Transit (BRT), now in successful operation in cities around the world—with particular success in South America—should be considered a preferred mode because of its low cost, operational flexibility, short construction time, capacity for phased implementation, and effective transit service. The anticipated lengths of the boulevard corridors, varying from a few miles to a dozen or more,[9] are ideally suited to BRT. In some cases, Light Rail Transit (LRT) may be a viable alternative (a light rail line has long been planned for Jerusalem). Though LRT typically has a higher per-mile cost, longer construction time, and less operational flexibility compared with BRT, these factors may be outweighed by other considerations such as population density, topography, technological issues, or local preference.[10]

Along the boulevards, uses could include newer housing, commercial areas, office buildings, mid-size hotels, government agencies, consulates, schools, and cultural facilities. Buildings would probably be taller than in the neighborhoods behind and might include mid-rise elevator buildings or even, where appropriate, high-rise buildings. Typical heights might be from five to ten stories. (See Figure 34.)

New Neighborhoods

At the heart of the proposal is the absorption of more than 2 million people in new neighborhoods along the flanks of the new transit boulevards. Here the sequential, ongoing creation of new neighborhoods can be calibrated to the pace of population growth and refugee return.

The Arc concept does not presuppose any particular type, scale, or style of housing, although it is noted that a wide range of types currently exists in the West Bank and Gaza, and in the wider region. These range from freestanding homes with gardens, historic "hosh" courtyard houses, mixed commercial and residential buildings, and multi-

Figure 34. The Transit Boulevard: Linking New Neighborhoods. Along the proposed boulevards, the emerging transit mode known as Bus Rapid Transit (BRT) would offer low construction cost, short construction time, capacity for phased implementation, operational flexibility, and effective transit service. In some cases, Light Rail Transit (LRT) may be a viable alternative. The transit service then supports the development of new neighborhoods flanking the boulevards. Residents would generally live no further than a 15-minute walk from the boulevard.

Figure 35. Housing Types. The Arc concept does not presuppose any particular type, scale, or style of housing; a wide range already exists in the West Bank and Gaza, including freestanding homes with gardens, historic "hosh" courtyard houses, and multistory apartment blocks. The target average density could be achieved with an appropriate mix for each municipal area. In all cases, the use of sustainable design elements such as solar power and recaptured "gray" water would be encouraged.

Figure 36. New Neighborhoods: Livable, Sustainable, Integrated. Along the transit boulevards, the sequential, ongoing creation of new neighborhoods can be calibrated to the pace of population growth and refugee return. In addition to housing, the new neighborhoods would include shops, markets, schools, clinics, mosques and other religious structures, small parks, and cultural facilities. Typical building heights might range from two to six stories. Residents could walk to municipal public transit linking them to the national transport network.

story apartment blocks. The Arc concept is based on achieving the target average density of 30,000 people per square mile within the defined built-up areas; this can be achieved with a range of balanced housing types, as appropriate for each municipal area and as approved by local communities. (See Figure 35.)

In addition to housing, the new neighborhoods would include shops, markets, schools, clinics, mosques and other religious structures, small parks, and cultural facilities. Typical building heights might range from two to six stories. (See Figure 36.)

Based on a very preliminary review, it is our belief that there is sufficient buildable terrain for a boulevard between each of the new stations and historic centers to accommodate the two million new residents at the proposed average density of 30,000 people per square mile.[11] (See Figure 37.)

The remaining one million would be housed through increased density in the built-up areas around the core and through some voluntary location in the smaller towns.

It should be stressed that while these numbers reflect demographic estimates through 2020, the Arc is intended to create a framework that can absorb Palestinian population growth and urban development over the long term. The combined tactics of urban density, public transit, and protected open space should be capable of supporting a sustainable, livable environment for generations. This proposition will need testing by Palestinian planners looking at 30-, 50-, or even 100-year scenarios for urban development. Key questions will be the capacity of the urban areas to increase densities, above and beyond this project's targeted average of 30,000 people per square mile within built-up areas. A doubling of densities to 60,000, for example, would double the potential for population absorption, still fall within acceptable ranges of sustainable density, and require no additional land. Long-term strategies for such increased densities—for example, through different housing types and patterns—should be investigated. In addition, planners may want to look at alternative approaches such as the expansion of the urbanized areas or the eventual introduction of one or more entirely new towns along the Arc infrastructure.

Historic Core

While growth is anticipated from the historic core toward the station area, investment and economic activity are in effect generated in the opposite direction, from the station to the historic core. National investment is pumped up and down the Arc and then diverted locally from the station area, along the boulevard, and into the historic core. This new investment brings life to ongoing efforts, particularly in the West Bank, to

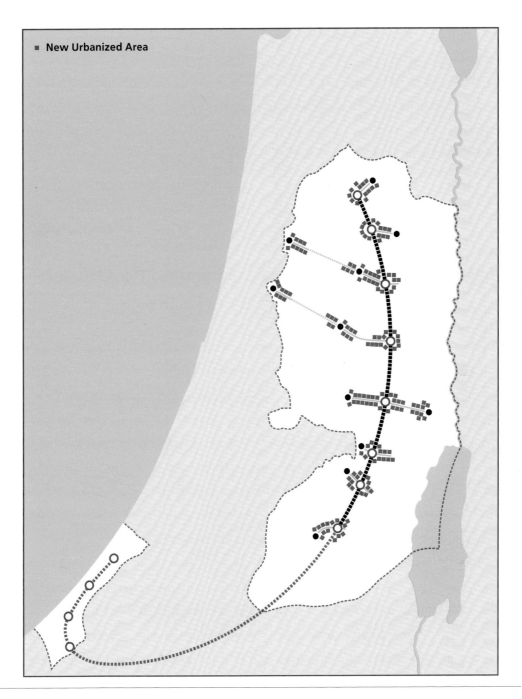

Figure 37. Linear Urban Growth. Within each municipal area, the establishment of the two poles of the historic center and the Arc station linked by the new transit boulevard provides the basic framework for accommodating population growth and urban expansion within the West Bank. Along the boulevard, new neighborhoods can be developed sequentially to accommodate as many as 3 million people in the next 15 years. The pattern thus directs urban growth while ensuring protection of the national open space system.

document, preserve, and adaptively reuse the historic buildings and spaces of the old cores. (See Figure 38.)

Housing in the historic core may be higher-density traditional courtyard housing combined with newer structures. Other uses could include ceremonial centers, libraries, museums, mosques, churches, schools, clinics, parks and public squares, markets, small hotels, and historic sites. Typical building heights might range from one to four stories. (See Figure 39.)

International Infrastructure: Trade, Tourism, and Transportation

Much of the Arc concept is focused on encouraging sustainable growth and critical linkages within the West Bank and Gaza. But the proposed formal structure has also been developed with an eye on its capacity to foster essential relationships with the world outside of the new state. In the area of trade, the Arc is intended to foster the ready movement of goods to and from the airport, seaport, and key border crossings—these are addressed below. With respect to tourism, it is noted that international tourism has become an essential part of the economy for most nations, particularly in and around the Mediterranean. A new Palestinian state should be no exception, not only because of its favorable location, but because of the beauty of its natural landscape, climate, and exceptional richness in sites of archeological, cultural, historic, and religious interest. (See Figure 40.) Good links between air and ground transportation are fostered by the Arc, as well as the provision of good public transportation service throughout the new country. The infrastructure of tourism—notably hotels and restaurants—should develop most naturally in the historic centers of Palestinian cities, whose accessibility, rehabilitation, and revitalization are primary goals of the Arc structure.

Roadways

While a rail line would be the centerpiece of the national infrastructure, rail cannot provide all the needed types of transport. On the passenger side, there will always be a demand for swift automobile linkages via highway—not only for those residents who can afford a car but also for tourists, dignitaries, government officials, etc. The demand will also exist for the providers of emergency services, security and military units, and service and repair vehicles of all kinds. On the freight side, although rail freight should

Figure 38. Revitalizing the Historic Cores. A key premise of the Arc is that the historic Palestinian urban centers are of vital cultural and economic importance to a new Palestinian state. The fundamental approach is to protect and revitalize the centers by linking them to new infrastructure at an appropriate distance. Economic activity all along the boulevard from the new station area to the old center should bring fresh investment to the historic areas, with an emphasis on the preservation and adaptive reuse of significant historic structures and districts.

Figure 39. Aerial View of Growth Sequence in Prototypical Municipal Area. The series of aerial views shows a possible sequence of growth and development—infrastructure, neighborhoods, and open space—within a single prototypical municipal area. The large aerial view shows the fully realized plan, including the transit boulevard (blue), starting from the historic center (upper left) and extending to the new station area (lower right). Also visible are historic Route 60 (along the top) and the new rail, water, energy, road, and park infrastructure along the line of the Arc.

ideally be incorporated into the Arc (see the sections on the airport and seaport), a significant percentage of freight is likely to be carried by truck, from small shipments in vans to shipping containers directly offloaded onto tractor-trailers. This freight traffic will require good roads as well.

The most typical response to demands of a growing number of motorized vehicle trips is to construct a network of multilane highways. But there are considerable risks and disadvantages to this approach. These roads are arguably the most expensive form of transport infrastructure; they also take the longest time to build. An emphasis on highways may therefore dominate whatever transportation funding is available, leaving a diminished budget for public transit. If highways become the dominant form of infrastructure, automobiles will likely become the dominant mode of travel. This leads to high consumption of costly fossil fuels and to air pollution. It creates enormous problems for urban development with respect to the voracious space demands to accommodate the automobile, both when moving and when parked. And most damaging of all, the highway infrastructure itself, particularly when designed in typical form with frequent entry and exit points, creates the conditions for urban sprawl. Urban sprawl would characteristically undo efforts to maintain compact urban form, undermine the effectiveness of public transit, increase average distances between residence and workplace, and threaten the survival of agricultural land and open space between cities.

We suggest, therefore, that one solution along the Arc would be the creation of a toll road with fewer rather than more lanes, and with very limited exit and entry points, perhaps one or two for each urban center. This would accommodate the national trucking requirements, as well as necessary service travel and optional automobile travel, without favoring the car to the extent that it dominates the urban form and infrastructural pattern of the whole country. The north-south Trans-Israel national toll road—now nearly completed—is arguably an example of what not to do: a multilane highway without companion public transportation, a construction funding strategy predicated on an ever growing number of motorists, and an interchange pattern that is likely to extend urban sprawl.[12]

We suggest that the toll-road exit and entry points be located quite close to but slightly removed from the station areas of the national rail line on the Arc. If too close, the vehicular movement will create excessive congestion at the station, where transverse movement from the municipal area will also need access. At the same time, one side of the station area may be appropriate for light industrial areas. These should be kept close enough to the local transit spine to allow people to walk to work and still provide ready access for truck traffic into and out of the industrial area.

Figure 40. Tourism. International tourism has become an essential part of the economy for most nations, particularly in and around the Mediterranean. A new Palestinian state should be no exception, not only because of its favorable location, but because of the beauty of its natural landscape, climate, and exceptional richness in sites of archeological, cultural, historic, and religious interest.

Airport

An international airport connecting Palestine to the rest of the world is assumed to be of critical importance in building both the identity and economy of the new state. (See Figure 41.) We have further assumed throughout this report that for reasons of security, the major Palestinian airport will necessarily be located in Gaza, rather than the West Bank.[13] Indeed, the current Palestine airport, though not operational, is located near Rafah in Gaza. From the perspective of infrastructure, habitation, economic development, and urban design, the Gaza location has both disadvantages and advantages. The primary disadvantage is that the significant majority of Palestinians now lives and will continue to live in the West Bank. The airport that will serve them will therefore be somewhat remote and in noncontiguous Gaza.

The current Rafah location is approximately 22 miles from the center of Gaza City. This falls right in the middle of typical airport-to-center-city distances for major international airports.[14] Most fall within the 15–30 mile range. At ten miles, Atlanta's airport is exceptionally close to downtown; at 37 miles, Tokyo's Narita is exceptionally far from central Tokyo. The Rafah airport would, in other words, offer normal benefits of proximity to Gaza City.

By contrast, Hebron, the closest large West Bank city, is 55 miles from Rafah along the proposed Arc; Jerusalem is approximately 70 miles. It is worth noting that Israel's primary airport, while only 12 miles from central Tel Aviv, is 31 miles from Jerusalem.

Nablus is 115 miles from Rafah, putting it at some disadvantage with respect to international linkages when compared with Hebron and Jerusalem. Needless to say, this calculus would change considerably if and when, at some future date, international relations improve to the point where Palestinians in the West Bank have the option of convenient access to air travel from airports in Israel and Jordan. Until such time, the southerly location of the airport pulls certain economic development southward and favors certain economic sectors in the more southerly urban areas.

The proposition that moderate or high-speed rail should be the primary purpose of the Arc is therefore based not only on linking the cities of the West Bank together and linking the West Bank to Gaza, but of spreading the benefits of proximity to the international airport more equitably across Palestine. If residents of Nablus could board a direct high-speed train to Rafah airport with a reliable scheduled travel time of 90 minutes or less, some of the city's potential isolation from international travel and commerce due to its northerly location may be mitigated. In the long term, Nablus might also benefit from its advantageous proximity to Haifa and its port, assuming improved neighborly relations.

Figure 41. Airport. An international airport connecting Palestine to the rest of the world is assumed to be of critical importance in building both the identity and economy of the new state.

With respect to contiguity, there is little doubt that the division of Palestine into two distinct areas separated by another sovereign nation creates its own set of problems to be overcome, with respect to both the function and identity of the new state. Other nations have dealt with this issue in different ways. Isolated West Berlin was served by rail service through an agreement in which the rail infrastructure was owned and controlled by East Germany, while the rolling stock itself belonged to West Germany. Though far from an ideal situation, the agreement did provide some measure of enhanced mobility to Berlin residents. In a perhaps more benign comparison, the land-mass of Denmark is composed mainly of a large peninsula (Jutland) and two large islands (Funen and Zealand). Though the peninsula and islands are separated by water rather than the territory of another national state, similar disadvantages of noncontiguity pertain. A trunk rail line linking Copenhagen on the west to the other major cities addresses these disadvantages. The high-speed rail trip from Copenhagen Airport to Odense is 115 miles (almost identical from Rafah Airport to Nablus) and takes only 72 minutes. This was accomplished thanks to the engineering feat of a tunnel and bridge across the water barrier of the Great Belt. The combination of infrastructure and transport service has thus overcome a major physical and psychological barrier. (See Figure 42.)

Finally, in addition to air passengers, the airport will certainly send and receive air cargo as well, and the Arc would be an important extension of the travel path for cargo, whether via small package shipping on passenger trains, larger shipments via rail freight, or shipments of any size on trucks using the toll road. Nonmanufacturing international companies increasingly depend on a reliable small-package shipping network. The Arc could offer the assurance of such a network for investment throughout most of Palestine.

Seaport

Another key international facility would be the seaport, south of Gaza City. As with the airport, this would serve both freight and passengers, although in this case freight would likely dominate. (See Figure 43.)

Maritime shipping would be a key area for investment in a Palestinian state and a critical part of its economic development. Though imports are likely to prevail at first, the eventual development of exporting industries and export products would depend upon a reliable shipping network. Because of the worldwide conversion to standardized container shipping, products to and from the seaport could be transported along the Arc either via container rail cars on a freight line running parallel to the passenger line, along the passenger line itself, or via container trucks operating along the parallel toll road.

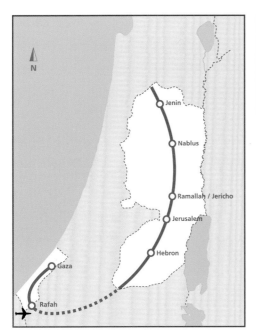

Figure 42. Danish Rail System as a Linking Infrastructure. Comparable to a prospective Palestinian state, Denmark is composed of separate land areas—primarily a peninsula and two islands. These are now linked by a high-speed rail line between Copenhagen and the other major cities (the trip from Copenhagen airport to Odense is 115 miles—almost identical to the distance from Rafah Airport to Nablus—and takes only 72 minutes). The final link across the Great Belt was accomplished by the engineering feat of building a rail tunnel and vehicular bridge.

Figure 43. Seaport. A seaport in Gaza would serve both freight and passengers. Maritime shipping would be a key area for investment in a Palestinian state. Though imports are likely to prevail at first, the eventual development of exporting industries and export products would depend upon a reliable shipping network. The port should also accommodate passenger ships and private vessels to help boost the tourism sector of the economy. The Arc could provide a convenient way for visiting passengers to make sojourns to the West Bank.

The port should also accommodate passenger ships and private vessels to help boost the tourism sector of the economy. The Arc could provide convenient access to and from sailing vessels from throughout the West Bank and Gaza, while offering a way for visiting passengers to make sojourns into the interior of the West Bank.

Land Gateways

While the Arc is initially intended to address internal linkages, it can ultimately provide the backbone for land travel and transport between the international capitals of Amman, Beirut, Cairo, and Damascus—and eventually Haifa and Tel Aviv. (See Figure 44.) International points of entry would be found at Jenin, Tulkarm, Qalqilya, south of Hebron, and east of Jericho. Infrastructure investment could be focused on linking these perimeters to the trunk of the Arc.

---

[1] "Virtues of the Compact City," *The Arizona Republic*, December 21, 2003.

[2] Yaakov Garb, "Sustainable Transport: Some Challenges for Israel and Palestine," *World Transport Policy and Practice*, Vol. 4, No. 1, 1998.

[3] The authors recognize that even a successful program to encourage and direct urban population growth to the West Bank is unlikely to reduce Gaza's rate of population growth to zero, desirable though this might be. Therefore, careful local planning within Gaza will be very important. Key decisions will include how much of the little remaining open space can be preserved, how to handle an inevitable increase of population density within existing built-up areas, and how to accommodate the increased movement of people and goods due to population increase and expanded economic activity from the airport and seaport. Because of Gaza's isolation and small land area, all these issues are viewed as falling within the province of the local planning authority. With respect to Gaza, the Arc concept is limited to providing a critical infrastructural link to the West Bank, as well as within Gaza.

[4] *Atlas of Palestine*, Jerusalem (Bethlehem): Applied Research Institute, 2002.

[5] The Central Highlands enjoy 300–800 mm (12–30 inches) of annual rainfall; that number drops quickly to 200 mm (8 inches) down to negligible on the arid eastern slopes.

[6] The status of the nine largest cities—Hebron, Bethlehem, Jerusalem, Jericho, Ramallah, Nablus, Qalqilya, Tulkarm, and Jenin—is beyond question. Tubas and Salfit are smaller but are consistently shown in the *Atlas of Palestine* as two of the eleven major cities. Furthermore, in the 11 administrative divisions adopted as "governates" by the Palestinian Authority in 1995, there is both a Salfit and Tubas governate, with each respective city its seat. Conversely, in the eight administrative divisions known as "districts," which the *Atlas of Palestine* shows more frequently, the Salfit and Tubas governates have been subsumed into the enlarged Nablus District, while the Qalqilya Governate has been subsumed into the enlarged Tulkarm District, leaving a total of eight districts rather than 11 governates.

[7] The Arc does favor nine of the major urban centers, somewhat to the disadvantage of two others, Qalqilya and Tulkarm. The prospects for development and growth in these two cities, tied closely to Israel because of their lower elevations and location directly on the border, must be weighed in relationship to the benefits of the internal north-south link. A somewhat longer alternative to the arc would be an S-form, which would swing westward before reaching Nablus—putting it closer to Qalqilya and Tulkarm—before curving back eastward to get to the Jenin area.

[8] RAND Corporation, Palestinian State Study Group, *Building a Successful Palestinian State*, Santa Monica, Calif.: The RAND Corporation, MG-146-DCR, 2005.

[9] Approximate proposed lengths of New Boulevard (in miles): Jenin—3, Tubas—3, Nablus—3, Tulkarm—12, Salfit—10, Qalqilya—12, Ramallah—6, Jericho—8, Jerusalem—3, Bethlehem—3, Hebron—3, Possible New Town—6. Total miles: 72.

[10] There is currently a vigorous debate within the world of professional transit planning as to the relative merits of BRT and LRT; many corridor "alternative" studies now focus primarily on weighing the choice between these two modes and determining their appropriateness for a specific corridor. There is also a growing technological convergence and even crossover between the two transport modes, for example train systems that operate on rubber tires, or bus systems with multi-door vehicles, overhead electric power, and automatic guidance systems.

[11] Each one mile of boulevard, assuming a 15-minute walk (3/4 mile) on either side, yields 1.5 square miles; thus 30,000 people × 1.5 = 45,000 people. To accommodate 3 million people, 66 miles of boulevards are needed. If one million people are assumed absorbed in the expansion and densification of the old cores, 2 million people need to be accommodated along the boulevard. Two million divided by 45,000 yields a need for 44 miles of boulevards.

[12] "Road to Ruin," *The Jerusalem Report*, July 10, 1997.

[13] However, if the Qalandia airport near Ramallah were to become operational again, it could be readily linked to the Ramallah/Jericho station.

[14] Airport-to-downtown distances (in miles, ascending order): Atlanta—10, New York (JFK)—12, Tel Aviv—12, Istanbul—15, London Heathrow—15, Amman—16, Paris (CDG)—16, Cairo—18, Chicago—18, Damascus—18, Denver—19, Hong Kong (Chep Lak Kok)—21, Riyadh—21, Rome—21, Washington (Dulles)—25, Milan Malpensa—27, London Gatwick—28, Jerusalem—31, Seoul (Incheon)—31, Tokyo (Narita)—37, London Stansted Airport—40.

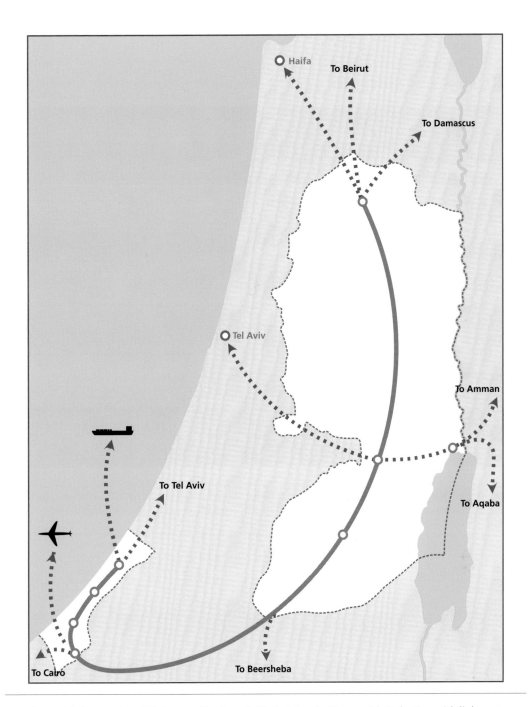

Figure 44. International Linkages. The Arc is initially intended to provide Palestine with linkages to domestic destinations and to the two critical international facilities—the airport and seaport. It should later provide the backbone for land travel and transport to Amman, Beirut, Cairo, and Damascus—and eventually Haifa and Tel Aviv. International points of entry would be found at Jenin, Tulkarm, Qalqilya, south of Hebron, and east of Jericho. Infrastructure investment could be focused on linking these international gateways to the trunk of the Arc.

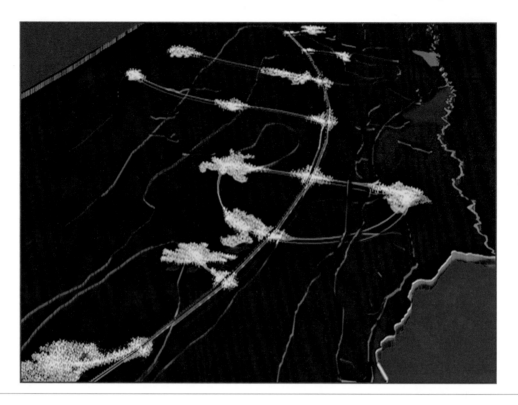

Nighttime Aerial View of the Arc. Nighttime view of the Arc in the West Bank, with Tulkarm, Qalqilya, and the Mediterranean (upper left), the Jordan Valley and Dead Sea (right), and Hebron (lower left).

Chapter Three

Costs and Economic Benefits

IN THIS SECTION, we estimate the construction costs associated with key elements of the Arc, particularly for transportation infrastructure and for additional housing associated with Palestinians settling in the West Bank and Gaza from abroad. In addition, we estimate the labor requirements for the construction of these elements. Given the current economic straits of the Palestinians, the number of jobs that would be created by major infrastructure development projects is important in its own right, in addition to the longer-term economic and social benefits of these projects.

Costs

We focus on construction costs in two areas: transportation—specifically a railroad and highway along the main length of the Arc, "boulevard" roads connecting the historical population centers to the train stations located on the Arc, the train stations themselves, and transit stations along the boulevard roads—and housing for immigrants to a new Palestinian state. We use a "parametric" method for estimating costs, in which we take information from analogous construction projects in other places (particularly Israel and Jordan) and adjust it to reflect the details of the Arc.[1]

Cost estimates in this section exclude the cost of land acquisition, whether for roads, railways, stations, or housing. This is because land acquisition costs were excluded from the available cost data from the analogous projects on which we base our cost estimates. We also note that land values are very difficult to ascertain, especially during such a period of stress and turmoil; may fluctuate dramatically over time; and, because a Palestinian government will likely have right of eminent domain, may be dictated by government decisions rather than land markets. In any case, we do not know how land acquisition costs would differ between Palestine and these analogous projects.

All the cost estimates in this chapter are intended as a frame of reference for considering the scale of infrastructure investment that would be required to implement the Arc concept, rather than as a precise budgeting tool. Detailed assessments of the costs of developing all the elements considered here will require site surveys, needs assessments, and much other work that was outside the scope of this project. However, estimates of the lengths of the various road and rail segments are accurate to one or two kilometers, based on the design of the Arc described in this book.

Our estimates of housing costs assume an influx of 630,000 people from Palestinian communities abroad, primary from Jordan and Lebanon (for reasons described in elsewhere in this chapter). If net migration is substantially higher or lower, the cost estimates will need to be adjusted accordingly.

Currently, housing in the West Bank and Gaza is considered to be crowded and of relatively poor quality.[2] Also, considerable new housing will be needed due to natural population growth, even in the absence of improvements in quality, reductions in crowding, or substantial immigration. However, determining these housing needs is outside the scope of this project.

Table 1 shows the components for which we have developed cost estimates and the estimates themselves: the railroad, including rolling stock; intermodal stations for both rail and bus passengers; the limited-access highway; the boulevards that connect the stations to the historical sectors; and the additional housing units.

Railways

Cost estimates for the railroad were taken from plans for an analogous project in Israel, the new Tel Aviv–Jerusalem railroad.[3] This railroad is similar to the one we describe for Palestine in this report: It is designed for rapid movement of large numbers of passengers and it has to climb a fairly steep grade from Tel Aviv to Jerusalem, similar to the changes in elevation in the Arc along the West Bank and Gaza. To estimate the costs of the Arc railway, we divided the total project cost of the Tel Aviv–Jerusalem railroad by its total length to calculate an average cost per mile ($21.27 million per mile for our base case estimate), and then multiplied this unit cost by the number of miles of the railroad along the Arc. The estimates for the railroad include the cost of aquiring passenger rolling stock.

In practice, the sources we found quoted a range for the total costs for the Tel Aviv–Jerusalem railroad. Our cost estimate in Table 1 is based on the high end of this range, as this was more consistent with other data on railroad construction costs for terrain similar to that in the West Bank and Gaza that we found from elsewhere in the world.

Highways and Boulevards

The costs of construction of the limited-access toll road are also based on cost estimates for an analogous Israeli project, the first leg of the Yitzhak Rabin cross-Israel Highway (Highway 6).[4] Like the proposed highway along the Arc, this highway is limited-access, grade-separated, and funded by tolls (at least in part); and it traverses various types of terrain.[5] As with the railway, more than one cost estimate was available for this project: the approximate actual costs of the first completed leg (which we chose for the basis of our estimate here, $13.41 million per mile); the projected high-end costs for the entire project; and a projected low-end cost for the entire project. Because construction projects are often susceptible to cost overruns, we chose the estimates based on actual as opposed to projected costs.

We note that RAND's related study, *Building a Successful Palestinian State*, includes discussion of the costs of constructing a secure connector road between Gaza and the West Bank in the context of an independent Palestinian state that includes these territories; the estimated cost per mile for this road, which was based on published analyses from Palestinian and Israeli sources, was comparable to the cost per mile we use here for the Arc highway.[6]

To estimate the cost of constructing the boulevards, or connecting roads, between the stations on the Arc and the historic city centers, we used information on the cost per mile of a 2004 World Bank project to construct a highway around the periphery of Amman, Jordan, $3.8 million per mile.[7]

Transportation Stations

To estimate the costs of the stations on the Arc, which will serve as transfer points between the main Arc railway and highways and the connecting boulevards to the historical city centers, we searched for information on analogous projects in Israel or other neighboring countries. We were unable to identify exactly analogous projects, but found information on the costs of constructing a new railway station in Jerusalem and new central bus stations in Haifa, Tiberius, and Jerusalem. The reported total cost for those projects ranged from $33 million for the Haifa bus station to around $50 million for the Jerusalem bus and train stations, respectively.[8] Each of these projects is similar in purpose and design to the stations on the Arc described in this report. In general, however, they are larger and have more capacity (e.g., buses/trains per day, number of passengers, and associated commercial space).[9] Also, the Jerusalem train station will be fully below ground.

In this context, we view the cost estimates for these projects as an upper bound for present purposes, and we base our cost estimates for the Arc on an assumed cost of $20 million per station (approximately half that of the various Israeli projects). We calculate the total cost of station construction by multiplying the assumed cost per station by the number of stations included in the Arc, i.e., nine in the West Bank and five in Gaza. As described in this chapter, the stations along the Arc are to be sized more or less equally, reflecting the emphasis on relatively even development and population growth in the cities. The stations need to be designed for substantial growth in traffic, and, as architectural symbols of the new Palestinian state, they also need to be architecturally inspiring. The cost estimates incorporate those two conditions.

In addition to the main train stations along the Arc, our design calls for "bus rapid transit" stations along the boulevards that connect the train stations along the Arc to the historic urban centers. Because of our experience with similar transportation systems elsewhere in the world, we estimate that these local stations will cost $250,000 each; we estimate the total cost by multiplying this figure by the total number of stations, assuming that there will be one station per two-thirds of a mile of boulevard road.

Housing

Housing is one of the largest investments made in any country. Across the globe, housing is the single largest investment made by most families, and the housing stock represents one of the largest components of a country's capital stock. Because of the costs of housing, only in rare instances do donors seek to cover the full construction costs

Table 1. Estimated Costs of Constructing Transport Links Along the Arc

COST ELEMENT	LENGTH/ NUMBER	UNIT COST (MILLIONS OF U.S. $)	ESTIMATED TOTAL COST (MILLIONS OF U.S. $)
Railroad (incl. rolling stock)	154 miles		
Principal estimate[a]		21.27 / mile	3,275
Secondary estimate[b]		11.50 / mile	
Stations – Rail[c]	14 stations	20.00 / station	280
Transit Boulevards[d]	72 miles	3.82 / mile	275
Stations - Boulevard[e]	108 stations	0.25 / station	27
Toll Road	154 miles		
Principal estimate[f]		13.41 / mile	2,065
Alternative estimate[g]		11.92 / mile	
Alternative estimate[h]		7.75 / mile	
Residential Housing[i]	100,000 units	0.025 / unit	2,500
Total			8,422

SOURCES (all web links as of January 6, 2005):
[a] "First Tender for Jerusalem-Modi'in Railway Published," *Globes* [online] (http://www.globes.co.il/serveen/), April 4, 2004.
[b] http://www.asiatradehub.com/israel/railways.asp#2 and http://www.jewishvirtuallibrary.org/jsource/Economy/transport.html.
[c] Bounded by data on the cost of new Jerusalem railway station ("New Jerusalem Railway Station Tender in 2005," *Globes* [online], December 21, 2003) and new central bus stations in Haifa ("Egged Inaugurates NIS 140m Haifa Bus Station," *Globes* [online], October 28, 2003) and Tiberius ("Nitsba, Batan to Build $40m Tiberias Mall, Hotel," *Globes* [online], 25 July, 2004).
[d] "Project Appraisal Document on a Proposed Loan in the Amount of U.S. $38.0 to the Hashemite Kingdom of Jordan for the Amman Development Corridor Project," Report Number 28251-JO, Washington, D.C.: World Bank, April 30, 2004, p. 12.
[e] Author's estimates.
[f] http://www.infoprod.co.il/country/israel1e.htm.
[g] http://www.asiatradehub.com/israel/roads.asp#2.
[h] http://www.roadtraffic-technology.com/projects/highway_6/specs.html (as of January 6, 2005).
[i] Bounded by data on home construction in the West Bank, 1995–1997 ("Staff Appraisal Report: West Bank and Gaza Housing Project," Report Number 15926-WBGZ, Washington, D.C.: World Bank, March 18, 1997, p. 2).

for expanding or improving housing stock. Assistance programs have found it more efficient to focus their efforts on reducing the administrative costs of obtaining building permits, establishing and registering titles, and improving credit and mortgage markets for housing.

In light of the experience of international assistance providers, we have assumed that most Palestinians will rely on their own efforts and resources to build or improve housing. At the same time, we recognize that a substantial influx of immigrants may have sufficiently large effects on local housing markets that donors may want to mitigate these effects. We therefore estimate the costs of constructing new housing for returnees. Assuming the same density of residents per dwelling as currently exists in Gaza and the West Bank (6.4 people per unit[10]), and our projection of a potential 630,000 returnees over ten years, an additional 100,000 housing units would be needed to house this influx.

To estimate costs, we first looked at costs of new housing in the West Bank and Gaza from the pre-Intifada period. During the 1995–1997 period, the price of new residences was between $40,000 and $100,000.[11] However, these prices were biased upwards because much of the construction in that period was for larger, better-quality units for professional and upper-income families. Prices were also inflated because of pent-up demand stemming from the difficulties in constructing new housing in the period before the Oslo Accords. Our second approach was to look for normative prices: costs of housing that the Palestinian authorities assume would be provided to lower-income returnees. In consultation with the Palestinian Authority, the same World Bank report cited above used a target range of $20,000 to $30,000 per unit in the preparation and design of a World Bank housing policy loan for the West Bank and Gaza.[12] We used the midpoint of this range, $25,000, for our calculations. We lacked adequate information to adjust for changes in construction costs since the publication of the report in 1997 and today, and thus did not attempt to do so.

Direct Economic Benefits of Infrastructure Construction

The construction of transportation infrastructure and housing would employ Palestinian construction workers, increasing employment and family incomes. We have estimated the potential number of construction jobs generated by this spending by dividing the total value of projected construction spending in dollars by an estimate of gross construction output per worker in dollars derived from employment and national income accounting statistics from neighboring Arab states. We first obtained statistics on employment in construction and gross output of the construction industry from Jordan's Department of Statistics for the most recent year available (1996).[13] We then divided gross output by employment to compute output per worker in dollars. We then divided the total value of projected construction spending by this number to compute person-years of employment likely to be generated by the project.

With a total investment of $8.417 billion (see Table 1), roughly 531,500 person years of construction labor would be needed to complete the projects described here, according to Jordanian data. Using analogous data for Egypt, where labor productivity in construction is lower than in Jordan, employment would account for 800,000 person years.[14] Assuming these projects would be built over a five-year time span, this investment would employ 100,000 to 160,000 Palestinians per year for five years.

---

[1] Parametric and other cost estimation methods are discussed in further detail in Chapter 1 of RAND's related study, *Building a Successful Palestinian State*.

[2] Palestinian Central Bureau of Statistics, "Health Survey—2000, Main Findings"; also Palestinian Central Bureau of Statistics, http://www.pcbs.org/phc_97/phc_t23c.aspx (as of January 1, 2005).

[3] http://www.jewishvirtuallibrary.org/jsource/Economy/transport.html (as of January 1, 2005).

[4] httpwww.infoprod.co.il/country/israel1e.html (as of January 1, 2005).

[5] The Cross-Israel Highway includes more lanes (6–10) than our design for the Arc highway, and it may also contain more interchanges per metropolitan area. At the same time, the route of the Arc highway involves generally higher and more varied terrain than that of the Cross-Israel Highway.

[6] The costs were $13.3 million per mile in *Building a Successful Palestinian State* compared to $13.41 million per mile used in this report (See Chapter Nine of *Building a Successful Palestinian State*).

[7] "Project Appraisal Document on a Proposed Loan in the Amount of U.S. $38.0 million to the Hashemite Kingdom of Jordan for the Amman Development Corridor Project," Report Number 28251-JO, Washington, D.C.: World Bank, April 30, 2004, p. 12. We note that the Amman ring road is designed as a grade-separated, limited-access road, while the boulevard roads in our design would be neither. At the same time, the areas to be traversed by the boulevard roads are typically more developed; also, the boulevard construction would be accompanied by construction of other infrastructure, such as water and sewer mains and power lines, which are not part of the Amman ring road design.

[8] "New Jerusalem Railway Station Tender in 2005," *Globes* [online], December 21, 2003; "Egged Inaugurates NIS 140m Haifa Bus Station," *Globes* [online], October 28, 2003; "Nitsba, Batan to Build $40m Tiberias Mall, Hotel," *Globes* [online], 25 July 25, 2004; "Nitsba, Amot Complete Leasing of Jerusalem Mall," *Globes* [online], March 4, 2001.

[9] For instance, the Tiberius bus station project includes a 14,000-square-meter mall, a 400-space underground parking garage, and a hotel; the bus station itself will be 800 square meters.

[10] Palestinian Central Bureau of Statistics, "Health Survey—2000, Main Findings"; also Palestinian Central Bureau of Statistics, http://www.pcbs.org/phc_97/phc_t23c.aspx (as of January 1, 2005).

[11] "Staff Appraisal Report: West Bank and Gaza Housing Project," Report Number 15926-WBGZ, Washington, D.C.: World Bank, March 18, 1997, p. 2.

[12] "Staff Appraisal Report: West Bank and Gaza Housing Project," Report Number 15926-WBGZ, Washington, D.C.: World Bank, March 18, 1997, p. 9.

[13] Department of Statistics of the Hashemite Kingdom of Jordan, http://www.dos.gov.jo/dos_home_e/main/index.htm (as of January 6, 2005).

[14] Employment data for the Egyptian construction sector were obtained from International Labour Office, *Key Indicators of the Labour Market, 2001–2002*, New York: Routledge, 2002, p. 180. We were unable to find gross output data for the construction sector for Egypt. However, we used the same ratios between gross output and value-added in the construction sector in Jordan to estimate gross output for the Egyptian construction sector from Egyptian data on value-added in the construction sector. The value-added data for the Egyptian construction sector were taken from the Statistics Division of the United Nations Department of Economic and Social Affairs, http://unstats.un.org/unsd/snaama/selectionbasicFast.asp.

CHAPTER FOUR

Sociopolitical Challenges

REFUGEE ABSORPTION IN PALESTINE[1] will involve both significant infrastructural and human elements. Many of the infrastructural challenges are discussed elsewhere in this book, as well as in our earlier companion volume.[2] Such challenges include the availability of water, housing, employment, and land on which to settle both returning refugees and the rapid natural population growth inside Palestine. Successful refugee absorption in Palestine must likewise overcome numerous intangible obstacles that are social and political in nature. Inattention to potential sociopolitical cleavages would likely make refugee absorption even more daunting and problematic than it already is. The purpose of this chapter is to outline nine sociopolitical challenges to refugee absorption that policymakers inside and outside Palestine must address in order to maximize the chances of success. Failure to successfully confront these challenges may imperil the success of the Palestinian state itself.

This study avoids the contentious issue of a Palestinian "right of return" to Israel itself simply because it is not directly relevant to refugee absorption in Palestine.[3] The number of returning refugees to Palestine will depend in large measure on the circumstances of their return and the level of success of a Palestinian state. For example, it is possible that Palestinian refugees in Lebanon may be compelled to return to Palestine or otherwise leave Lebanon, while those in Jordan may have the luxury of waiting to see how successful the state is before deciding whether or not to immigrate. Similarly, a Palestine that is economically viable and productive, where jobs and housing are available, and where governance is good will likely attract far higher numbers of returning refugees than would a Palestine without such opportunities.

While the actual level of refugee return will depend on several variables and cannot be predicted with a high level of confidence, the best estimates suggest a return to the Palestinian state of between 500,000 and 1,000,000 migrants.[4] These estimates are consistent with reported plans by the Palestinian Authority (PA) to absorb approximately 700,000 refugees under a peace settlement. In addition, Palestine's natural population growth—among the highest in the world—may produce another 1 million souls in less than a decade. Thus, the challenge to the state of Palestine and, by extension, the international community, to effectively absorb such a large population increase without endangering the viability of the new state itself is acute.

In addition to the absolute number of refugees migrating to Palestine, the time frame for migration is also critical. Absorbing 500,000 refugees in the first two years of statehood poses far more risks to the stability of the new state than the same level of migrants absorbed over ten years. Refugee absorption that is well organized and drawn out over a period of years will better serve the stability of Palestine, and the region, than a chaotic and rushed migration to the new state.

There are virtually no hard data on the *type* of refugee most likely to migrate to Palestine, although there is a great deal of anecdotal information and informed speculation.[5] That speculation largely assumes that poorer and less educated Palestinians will be most likely to migrate to Palestine, especially those based in Lebanon. Unlike Jordan, Lebanon has exercised significant discrimination against Palestinian refugees, making education, housing, employment, and general societal integration highly problematic. The result has been both a high level of secondary and undocumented migration (to the Gulf primarily) and a remaining and destitute population ill-suited for smooth absorption into any state, much less a brand new state of Palestine.

State Legitimacy and Refugee Absorption

The most important political issue surrounding refugee absorption is its impact on the legitimacy of the new state in the eyes of Palestinians. Refugee absorption will be a double-edged sword for which there will be no easy policy solution. On the positive side, in Palestinian historiography, the very raison d'etre of the new state will be to end the suffering and dispossession of the Palestinian people that, began with the "nakba," or catastrophe, of Israel's founding in 1948. In this regard, large-scale refugee absorption represents an integral part of the state's existence. The successful and large-scale absorption of Palestinians thus becomes a key litmus test for the legitimacy of the new state.

On the negative side, however, a Palestinian state that invites a massive and rapid return of the poorest and least educated Palestinians will put its own viability as a state at risk. Such a return will likely swamp Palestine's infrastructural and institutional capacities, make rapid economic development more difficult, and risk the rise of a "failed state" of Palestine, thereby delegitimizing the new state in the eyes not only of many Palestinians but of the international community as well.

The government of Palestine will therefore need to play an adept balancing game. It will need to be seen as solving the refugee problem, but it cannot absorb too many Palestinians too quickly without risking state collapse. Palestine will need to have an open immigration policy but at the same time limit immigration in three ways. First, while the poorest Palestinians will likely be the most eager to migrate, Palestine will need to encourage immigration for middle class Palestinians who have both the skills and the capital to help Palestine succeed. Second, it will be essential that annual immigration quotas be adopted to prevent a massive and chaotic return to Palestine. The practical implication of such quotas is that some eager returnees may have to wait several years or longer to migrate to Palestine, thereby engendering discontent and political problems for the new government. Third, Palestine must be prepared to cap total immigration without being seen as doing precisely that. Refugee absorption and natural population growth will likely increase the total population of Palestine by about 50 percent during the first decade of statehood, from about 3.5 million to about 5.25 million people. It is unclear how the new state will be able to successfully manage such a massive population increase. Limiting refugee absorption may well be the price Palestine must pay in order to succeed as a state.

Sociopolitical Tensions In Refugee Absorption

While most of this study deals with "hard" infrastructural issues related to successful population absorption, there are a number of important "soft" sociopolitical issues that ought not be ignored by planners. We outline nine such issues below. Clearly, some of these issues are more consequential than others, but all could have significant deleterious effects on Palestine if they are not handled correctly. Some of these potential tensions have no obvious and easy political solution.

1. Democracy and Institutional Capacity

Samuel Huntington argued in his seminal book *Political Order in Changing Societies* that fragile political institutions of new states in the decolonized world could easily be overrun by rapid increases in politically aware and mobilized populations. Political institutions in new states simply lacked the capacity to respond to rapidly increasing demands made on them. For Huntington, this meant that democracy was an unlikely political outcome in the near term in these states and, indeed, premature democratic inclusion would likely occur only at the expense of stability and economic development.[6]

We are not as pessimistic about democracy in Palestine as Huntington's old argument would perhaps suggest. Indeed, in the companion volume to this present study, we argue for the political advisability of democracy in Palestine from the outset of statehood.[7] However, there is little doubt that large-scale refugee absorption in Palestine will pose a similar threat to fragile political institutions as Huntington argued. Weak and often new institutions—village councils, municipal governments, national government, the judicial system, etc.—will be strained to deal with a sudden increase in the population of perhaps 50 percent.

Under such strain, it will be tempting for the government of Palestine to suspend democracy and rule under some form of martial law. This would be a major mistake that the international community ought not support. For reasons laid out in our other volume, authoritarianism in Palestine would be especially difficult to reverse and would likely lead to poor economic performance, little political accountability, continued corruption, and diminished investment in Palestine.

This then, is the first major tension: To be successful as a state, Palestine must represent the will of the people and be democratic; but refugee absorption may imperil that objective by overwhelming fragile state institutions.

Well-planned, spread out, and limited refugee absorption may enhance the prospects for democracy in Palestine or, at the very least, not undermine them. In addition, widespread Palestinian knowledge of and support for democracy may assist in creating a democratic culture in Palestine that is better able to tolerate institutional weakness without resort to authoritarian policies.

2. Carrying Capacity

The total population any given region and its resources can sustain is known as the carrying capacity of that region. A carrying capacity is not a fixed number because economic prosperity can sharply raise the total carrying capacity of a region over time. While Gaza and Hong Kong have similar population densities, Hong Kong's economic wealth allows it to sustain a high population density at a much higher standard of living than that found in Gaza.

Due to scarce resources and a relatively rudimentary economy, Palestine is likely approaching its carrying capacity at near current economic activity. However, given the vagaries of occupation, it is hard to gauge what the actual carrying capacity might be. More important, significant post-independence investment and economic productivity will ideally considerably increase Palestine's total carrying capacity. In the near term, however, shortages of water, land, and wealth likely limit Palestine's ability to successfully absorb significantly higher population numbers.

The absorption of large numbers of refugees may prove to be an economic boon over the long term. However, large-scale immigration of the poorest and least educated Palestinians will likely prove to be a significant drain on scarce resources in the near term, and negatively impact prospects for economic growth. Herein lies the second tension for Palestine: In order to effectively increase its ability to carry a greater population, Palestine must experience significant economic growth; however, in order to maximize the chances for economic growth, Palestine must limit large-scale refugee absorption or other forms of rapid population increase.

3. Refugees and Non-Refugees

A sharp political cleavage exists in Palestinian society between those with refugee status and those who are not refugees. Since virtually all Palestinians in the diaspora are refugees,[8] this cleavage is particularly relevant inside the West Bank and Gaza. Simply put, refugees have a lower social status than non-refugees. The Israeli journalist Amira Hass captured this distinction well in the following vignette from Gaza:

Abu Majed's home is in Gaza City's Nasser neighborhood, where refugees and muwataneen (non-refugees) live side by side. Four years ago, his daughter reached school age and was about to start at the UNRWA (United Nations Relief and Works Agency) school for refugees. "We'll be able to walk together," she told a friend happily. The friend, the daughter of a muwataneen, replied haughtily, "No, we won't. You're a muhajera, a refugee. You have to go to school in the camp." "That was the first time she'd heard the word," Abu Majed said, "and she came to ask me what it meant. She thought the girl was cursing at her. I told her that it's an honor to be called a refugee. . . . Sometimes we feel like the gypsies in Europe, like people without respect. If one of us wants to marry a Gazan girl, the first thing they say is that he's a refugee. That hurts.[9]

The social cleavage between refugees and non-refugees does not appear to be diminishing significantly, especially since intermarriage between the two groups remains rare. For example, in 1995, only 9.2 percent of all marriages in Gaza were between refugees and non-refugees.[10] On the other hand, public opinion survey data indicate that on key issues, refugees and non-refugees in Palestine think alike and that there seems to be no "refugee identity."

Significant refugee absorption in Palestine would likely exacerbate social tensions between refugees and non-refugees. This is especially true in the West Bank, where most, and perhaps all, refugee absorption would need to take place. Currently, refugees number just over 600,000 souls in the West Bank, or about 30 percent of the total West Bank Palestinian population, and about 850,000, or nearly 60 percent of the Gaza population. In total, refugees make up just over 40 percent of the total Palestinian population in the West Bank and Gaza. Refugee absorption in the range contemplated by the PA and in this report would make refugees a majority of the total Palestinian population in the West Bank and Gaza, at about 55 percent.[11] It is to be expected that such a shift in population demographics will engender resentment on the part of non-refugees, especially given that resources will likely flow in greater abundance to refugees in Palestine. The political consequences of non-refugee resentment at the large influx of refugees in the West Bank may well be significant.

An overlapping cleavage concerns "insiders" (mixed refugees/non-refugees) and Palestinian "outsiders" (all refugees). We have already seen how such a cleavage can have negative political consequences. The PA, established in 1994, was fundamentally an organization of "outsiders"—Palestinian Liberation Organization officials and their supporters who came from Tunis to Palestine following the signing of the first Oslo Accord in 1993. The rule of the "Tunisians" generated significant ill-will among the existing West Bank/Gaza population, and helped lead to the creation of an authoritarian polity marked by corruption.[12] We expect similar political resentments will be generated during and following a significant refugee influx into Palestine.

Thus, a third tension is this: In order for refugee absorption to be successful, Palestine will need to have the majority non-refugee population willingly agree to become a minority population in a country that would then have a majority refugee population.

4. Refugees from Different Host Countries

Another concern for policymakers will be the potential tension between refugees arriving from different host countries. In the Palestinian diaspora, Jordan, Lebanon, and Syria have played host—for over 50 years—to most Palestinian refugees. Jordan currently has 1.7 million registered Palestinian refugees (and hundreds of thousands of "displaced persons" and other Palestinians), while Lebanon and Syria each have nearly 400,000 registered refugees.[13] The conditions in which each of these three refugee communities lives have been remarkably divergent. Conditions in Lebanon have been particularly bad, with Palestinians not only denied Lebanese citizenship, but denied most employment and educational opportunities as well. 56 percent of Palestinian refugees living in Lebanon still live in refugee camps, compared to only 17 percent in Jordan and 28 percent in Syria. Conversely, Jordan has extended citizenship rights to Palestinians, and has allowed the community to prosper through its domination of Jordan's private economic sector. While there are clear red lines for Palestinians in Jordan when it comes to political activities, they have been free to pursue other avenues of social and economic interest. Syria represents something of a midrange point between Lebanon and Jordan in terms of treatment of Palestinian refugees: they have not been granted Syrian citizenship, but otherwise have similarly low levels of economic and political opportunities as Syrian citizens.

What is not clear is how well these communities—separated for three generations—will intermingle once they return to Palestine. Should Palestine plan to absorb these refugees as groups, for example, housing most refugees from Lebanon in the same areas, or should planners aim to mix the communities in resettlement areas? Given that refugees in each host country tend to come from the same geographic and familial units, there will be a natural inclination for these refugees to resettle together in Palestine. To do so, however, would perpetuate political cleavages of, for example, "Lebanese Palestinians" or "Syrian Palestinians." This, then, is a fourth tension in resettlement: To allow completely free choice of resettlement location in Palestine would perpetuate sociopolitical cleavages based on host country, but to compel the dispersal of extended familial units may create significant political discontent.

5. Status of West Bank–Gaza Refugees

Policymakers often think in terms of resettling Palestinian refugees who would return to Palestine from one or another host Arab country. However, the West Bank and Gaza currently house 1.5 million registered refugees, of whom 625,000 still live in camps. Since these refugees already live in Palestine, will they be eligible for the resources allocated to refugee resettlement for those returning from, for example, Lebanon? To ignore the pressing needs of refugees already present in Palestine would likely create high levels of animosity against the returning refugees for whom resources are available, including new housing. This would particularly be true for refugees in Palestine still living in the camps.[14] It may also be a problem for registered refugees in Palestine who no longer live in camps. Some of these Palestinians are reasonably well off, while many are not. Will they be able to participate in a resettlement program? If not, they can seriously threaten the legitimacy of the state. This is a fifth tension to consider: To exclude refugees already present in Palestine from resettlement opportunities would generate resentment among those refugees against the returning refugees; but to include them will make more expensive any resettlement program at a time of diminishing international interest to allocate more resources to this issue.

6. Refugees Versus Displaced Persons

Legally speaking, Palestinian refugees are those people displaced during the 1948 war and who subsequently registered with the UN. Their dependents are also considered refugees. If a Palestinian was displaced prior to the 1948 war or in a subsequent war or event, he or she is not classified as a refugee. This distinction is particularly important in light of the 1967 war, when approximately 370,000 Palestinians were expelled or otherwise displaced from the West Bank and Gaza and moved into Jordan. Most Palestinians made homeless during the 1967 war are legally considered "displaced persons," not refugees. Interestingly, 113,000 Palestinians are classified as both refugees and displaced persons.[15] These were Palestinians expelled from their homes in what became Israel in 1948, generally settling in the West Bank—thereby classified as refugees—who were exiled a second time in 1967, thereby qualifying as displaced persons as well. In sum, the 1967 war produced approximately 260,000 displaced persons and an additional exodus of 113,000 Palestinians already defined as refugees.

Unlike the UN registering mechanism used for the 1948 refugees, no such mechanism was in place for the 1967 displaced persons, so the exact numbers are less clear. That said, displaced persons and their descendents today number approximately 800,000. Israel has been more willing to allow displaced persons to return under family reunification permits than refugees.

The Shikaki poll gauging the numbers of Palestinians that would likely migrate to Palestine under specified conditions did not distinguish between refugees and displaced persons, so the general range of returnees (500,000–1,000,000) is unaffected by this distinction. However, it is quite possible that policymakers will give priority to one category of Palestinian—likely refugees—when it comes to refugee absorption. To do so would create a new cleavage among Palestinians that up to this point has only been important in legal and academic studies: that between refugee and displaced person. This is a sixth potential tension for policy makers to consider: Giving priority to the resettlement of refugees may create resentment among displaced persons—who are, in fact, refugees in all meaningful ways but legal classification.

7. To Where Do the Refugees Return?

The vast majority of Palestinian refugees come from what is now the state of Israel. It is likely that few of these refugees will be able to resettle in their home villages in Israel. Those Palestinians who return will likely be resettled in the West Bank, Gaza, and any lands "swapped" as part of a final settlement. In other words, Palestinians will not be returning to home villages, but "returning" to areas in which they have no family history. Families originally from Haifa may be resettled in Hebron; those from Jaffa may end up in Jericho.

While the national Palestinian leadership may accept this "diverted return" as a necessary step toward acquiring statehood, and, indeed, many returning Palestinians generations removed from their "home" village may be comfortable with it as well, there will likely be political ramifications in a situation of not-quite-returned Palestinians. The biggest concern is that these Palestinians become a source of perpetual contention vis-à-vis the government of Palestine, and even irredentism vis-à-vis Israel. This concern would be especially grave under circumstances in which the government of Palestine is performing poorly economically and/or politically. This is a seventh tension: In order to be seen as successful, the state of Palestine must absorb refugees as part of a final status agreement that addresses the refugee issue; however, those very same absorbed refugees would be a likely source of political discontent given that they will likely not be returned to their familial home villages and towns and will likely congregate together and possibly form enclaves of discontent.

8. Refugees Who Do Not Return

Not all Palestinian refugees will choose to return to Palestine for resettlement upon the establishment of a Palestinian state. It is expected that many Palestinians in Jordan who have Jordanian citizenship and are relatively well off economically will chose to remain in Jordan.[16] Palestinian refugees in the Gulf states and elsewhere may seek Palestinian citizenship but likely will continue to reside in their current host countries. Other Palestinian refugees, especially some in Lebanon and Syria, may in part be resettled in a third country.[17] This combination of options—Palestinians resettled in Palestine, willingly resettled in a third country, or staying where they currently are for positive economic reasons—will likely account for the lion's share of all Palestinian refugees in the diaspora. However, it will not account for all exiled Palestinians.

It is likely that some Palestinians will choose to simply stay put awaiting the full "liberation" of Palestine that would allow them to return to their old family homes in Jaffa and elsewhere. Host governments may be unable or unwilling to compel repatriation to Palestine or full absorption domestically. Palestinians choosing to remain in exile under conditions of statehood will constitute a continuing source of instability for the new state of Palestine and a security risk for Israel. They will represent an authentic Palestinian voice of criticism, that the Palestinian Liberation Organization had "sold out" the rights of Palestinians, that it had settled for 23 percent of historic Palestine instead of all Palestine, that it had negotiated away their homes and villages.

If the number of Palestinians choosing to remain exiled in this way is high, the new state will have potentially serious problems of legitimacy and security. It will also make refugee absorption and resettlement more difficult because those Palestinians who choose a return to the state of Palestine will be accused of betraying the cause by those left behind. The state of Palestine has two conflicting interests in this regard. On the one hand, it has an interest in not being overrun by refugees, thereby putting at risk the viability of the new state. On the other hand, it has a political interest in ensuring that the "negative" diaspora community is as small as possible, thereby removing a potential source of perpetual criticism. This is an eighth tension: to keep to a manageable number the level of returnees, while at the same time making sure the number of Palestinians remaining in the diaspora for negative reasons is kept small. This tension cannot be resolved by Palestine alone, but must involve the active participation of the international community. Regional perceptions of the legitimacy of the final status agreement will be especially important in this regard.

9. From UNRWA to National Government

Registered Palestinian refugees have had various social services provided to them by UNRWA for over 50 years. These services include schooling and the provision of basic foodstuffs. In a real sense, UNRWA has served as a government agency for many Palestinians. Moreover, outside of Jordan, Palestinian refugees are typically "stateless" and have no representation by a national government. Stateless Palestinians, for example, do not have national passports with which to travel, but instead must use various forms of temporary travel documents—when they are available.

The consequence for Palestinian statehood is twofold. First, many Palestinians have no history of a relationship with a national government that provides for and protects its Palestinian citizens. At best, national government has been a bothersome inconvenience for many Palestinians, an entity that Palestinians must beseech periodically for various permits, but one that is always wary and skeptical. At worst, national government for Palestinians means an enemy, something that is to be feared and that will provide only permanent insecurity to Palestinians. Civil wars in Jordan and Lebanon, mass expulsion from Kuwait, and, of course, a long and hostile Israeli military occupation give Palestinian refugees reasons to fear national government.

Thus, many refugees being absorbed in Palestine will arrive with a predisposition that is at best skeptical of what it means to have a national government, and perhaps hostile to the sacrifices that a national government will demand of its citizens. These attitudes might also reflect a skepticism about democracy given that those returning from outside Palestine are likely to have been socialized in a political culture that is not democratic. The danger is that such views will reduce public demand for democracy. There will likely be a steep learning curve for many refugees before they accept and work with the government of Palestine. Significant anecdotal evidence suggests that the PA had the most difficulty in penetrating and gathering support from existing refugee camps in the West Bank and Gaza. This problem will be greatly magnified with significant refugee absorption.

A second and related problem concerns the culture of dependency that UNRWA has been accused of fostering.[18] UNRWA's mandate was and is to provide assistance to Palestinian refugees. The focus of its work has not been to create sustainable development and self-sufficiency among Palestinian refugees (for reasons that go far beyond what

UNRWA can control). Palestinian statehood will likely mean the end of UNRWA, but it probably does not mean the eradication of the culture of dependency that has grown up around UNRWA for the last five decades. Transforming this culture of dependency will be a major challenge for the government of Palestine. It may actually be made worse by the large amount of international aid that will likely flow into Palestine with a final settlement agreement with Israel.

A ninth sociopolitical challenge for Palestine will be to transform the twin cultures of hostility to national government and dependency for refugees seeking to settle in Palestine. Palestine will be able to afford neither a population largely distrusting of national authority or one mired in a culture of dependency.

Conclusion

Successfully resettling Palestinian refugees will be a raison d'etre for the new Palestinian state. However, absorbing hundreds of thousands of refugees, in conjunction with finding jobs and homes for one of the fastest growing populations on earth, will be fraught with dangers. This chapter summarizes sociopolitical tensions and challenges that will accompany refugee absorption and about which policymakers need to be concerned as they plan for creating a successful state. Some of these challenges are rather obvious, including the potential strains on state institutions and democracy, and the ability of Palestine's economy to effectively absorb a burgeoning population. Other challenges are less obvious but no less important, and include especially how the various "classes" of Palestinians are treated (refugee/non-refugee, insider/outsider refugees, refugees/displaced persons, Lebanon/Jordan/Syria refugees, etc.). The political ramifications of how well these challenges are addressed will likely be enormous, and will go far in determining the success of Palestine.

The nine sociopolitical challenges to successful refugee absorption discussed here are not, of course, the only challenges that Palestine will face on this issue, but they do include the most important ones. Palestine cannot approach refugee absorption—and large population growth in general—in a piecemeal fashion without jeopardizing the prospects for success of the new state. Rather, Palestine will need a comprehensive development plan that includes as a key component how refugees can be successfully resettled as well as plans for dealing with a rapidly expanding population. Without such advanced planning, Palestine could dissolve into chaos with the arrival of a million new immigrants at the birth of statehood.

---

[1] For the purposes of this study, Palestine is defined here as those parts of Mandate Palestine conquered by Israel in the 1967 war; that is, Gaza, West Bank, and East Jerusalem. The exact border between Israel and Palestine is subject to final status negotiations.

[2] *Building a Successful Palestinian State.*

[3] Palestinians maintain that refugees have a right to return to their homes and villages inside Israel and cite international humanitarian law and United Nations General Assembly Resolution 194 of 1949 to bolster their case. Israel has steadfastly refused to consider a large-scale influx of Palestinian refugees to Israel as part of a final settlement, arguing that such a return would threaten demographically the Jewish character of the state. For the purposes of this study, we assume that most returning refugees will be settled in Palestine, not Israel. This assumption is made for purely pragmatic reasons and does not indicate any position taken on the legal arguments concerning the "right of return."

[4] The best work on the question of refugee preferences for "return" can be found in a comprehensive survey led by Dr. Khalil Shikaki of the Palestine Center for Policy and Survey Research (PSR), available at http://www.pcpsr.org/survey/polls/2003/refugeesjune03.html. Refugees not emigrating to Palestine would stay in their host Arab countries or be resettled in third countries.

[5] A forthcoming study from PSR, "Policy Options for Absorbing Returning and Remaining Refugees to the Palestinian State," will include data not yet available to RAND. According to PSR, however, these data will confirm that returnees are likely to be poor and less well educated. On the other hand, they will indicate that the average family size will be somewhat smaller than is the case with Palestinians now in the West Bank and Gaza.

[6] Samuel P. Huntington, *Political Order in Changing Societies* (New Haven: Yale University Press, 1968, reissued 1996).

[7] *Building a Successful Palestinian State* (Santa Monica: RAND, 2005), Chapter 2.

[8] Some diaspora Palestinians never formally registered as refugees with UNRWA, while a small number of others did not meet the UN's definition of Palestinian refugee. In addition, Palestinian refugees (from the 1948 war) are legally distinguished from Palestinian "displaced persons" (refugees from the 1967 war). As a sociocultural matter, virtually all diaspora Palestinians view themselves as refugees; camp-dweller versus non-camp-dweller is a more potent cleavage in the diaspora.

[9] Amira Hass, *Drinking the Sea at Gaza: Days and Nights in a Land under Siege* (London: Hamish Hamilton, 1996) pp. 175–176, as quoted in Robert Bowker, *Palestinian Refugees; Mythology, Identity, and the Search for Peace* (Boulder: Lynne Rienner, 2003).

[10] Palestinian Authority figures. Quoted in Bowker, p. 70.

[11] Bowker, p. 72.

[12] For more detailed discussions of this phenomenon, see Glenn E. Robinson, *Building a Palestinian State: The Incomplete Revolution* (Bloomington: Indiana University Press, 1997), Chapter 7, and *Building a Successful Palestinian State*, Chapter Two.

[13] The actual refugee population in Lebanon is likely significantly less than the official numbers suggest due to unregistered migration elsewhere, primarily to the Gulf.

[14] Because these refugees are the closest geographically to Israel and Israel will have a perceived interest in the rapid dismantlement of the camps, the new government will be under pressure to integrate these refugees quickly.

[15] Bowker, p. 65.

[16] This assumes Jordan would allow Palestinians to remain in Jordan—something that is likely but not assured. There is a small Jordanian revanchist movement to expel Palestinians to Palestine once the state is established.

[17] For example, during the Oslo period there were persistent rumors that Canada had agreed to resettle a significant number of Palestinian refugees.

[18] For example, see Benjamin Schiff, *Refugees Unto the Third Generation* (Syracuse: Syracuse University Press, 1995).

CHAPTER FIVE

Conclusion

IF A STATE OF PALESTINE IS CREATED, it is essential that it succeed. The purpose of this book is to describe steps that Palestinians, Israelis, Americans, and the
international community can take to ensure that a new independent Palestinian state
is successful.

The research described in this book builds on a prior RAND study, *Building a
Successful Palestinian State*, which analyzed a wide range of political, economic, social,
and environmental challenges that a new Palestinian state would face and described
policy options in these areas for facilitating the state's success. In this study, we extend
the scope of analysis by providing a detailed vision for strengthening the physical infrastructure of a Palestinian state. This vision is designed to address one of the key challenges described in RAND's first study: building an adequate base of infrastructure to
foster the physical and economic well-being of Palestine's current and rapidly growing
population.

Every nation state has a shape, which is most immediately recognized by the contours of its international borders. Within those borders there is another shape that we
call the nation's formal structure—the pattern of constructed human habitation and
human movement, set in relationship to the natural environment. As we describe in
this book, the principal Palestinian urban centers are distributed along an arc running
from Jenin in the northern West Bank, through Hebron in the southern West Bank,

and then southwest to Gaza (the main exceptions to this are the West Bank cities of Tulkarm and Qalqilya, which lie to the west of the arc).

Based on this historical pattern of habitation, we develop a detailed vision for a modern, high-speed transportation infrastructure between the main Palestinian cities, which we refer to as the Arc. This transportation backbone accommodates substantial population growth in Palestine, by linking current urban centers to new neighborhoods via new linear transportation arteries that support both commercial and residential development. The Arc links Palestine to its neighbor states by road and rail, and to the rest of the world also by sea and air. The Arc preserves Palestinian green space, providing for an interconnected system of national parks and open land. And it avoids the environmental costs and economic inefficiencies of unplanned, unregulated urban development that might otherwise accompany Palestine's rapid population growth.

We recognize that no single construction project—even one as comprehensive as the Arc—could address all the political, social, and economic issues that a new Palestinian state will face. Very substantial challenges lie ahead. Furthermore, we emphasize that the details of the Arc design, as we present them in this book, are not a literal blueprint. Rather, they are intended as a starting point for discussion and planning of future Palestinian infrastructure development. Even if the fundamental concepts of the Arc were embraced, we would expect any realization to be influenced and inflected by local conditions and, as importantly, local preference. To succeed, a broad planning concept must not only be readily understood, but be widely accepted.

At the same time, we believe that infrastructure development of the scope and scale described here is a necessary, if not sufficient, condition for the success of an independent Palestinian state over its first decade. Moreover, it seems plausible that key aspects of the Arc design can be pursued, with great benefit, even before an independent Palestinian state is established. There is certainly a pressing need for such development, given current poor economic conditions and the fact that Palestinian infrastructure, inadequate even for current needs, must accommodate substantial and ongoing population growth.

Implementation of a program like the Arc will require strong and sustained political and financial commitments from the international community. In RAND's first report, *Building a Successful Palestinian State*, we describe scenarios of economic growth that assume levels of capital investment of around $3.3 billion per year, or a total of around $33 billion over the first decade of independence. That figure would accommodate most or all of the specific investment needs we describe in this book. Thus the approximately $6 billion needed to build the Arc's main transportation infrastructure represents 18 percent of the total discussed in RAND's first report, while the overall $8.5 billion cost of Arc infrastructure plus refugee housing represents about one-quarter of the ten-year total.

As a frame of reference for the magnitude of funding that may be required from international donors to ensure successful Palestinian development, we considered the cases of Bosnia and Kosovo, two areas where the international community has recently invested very large sums for post-conflict reconstruction. Like the West Bank and Gaza, these two entities suffered considerable damage from conflicts. Bosnia and Kosovo have not only attracted considerable international interest and assistance, both have had some success in creating democratic governments and revitalizing the local economies.

In per capita terms, the ten-year total of $33 billion in capital investment represents an annual average of approximately $760 per person. For comparison, this is about 2.5 times the amount of international aid per capita provided to the West Bank and Gaza in 2002 (approximately $300), less than twice the per capita amount provided to Kosovo in the first two post-conflict years ($433), and only slightly more than the per capita amount provided to Bosnia in its first two post-conflict years ($714).

Thus there are recent precedents for providing levels of international aid per capita that approach what we estimate will be needed in Palestine. At the same time, the level of international commitment we describe here and in RAND's other study is higher (in per capita and absolute terms), and is sustained over a longer period of time, than the assistance provided to Bosnia, Kosovo, or other major international aid efforts in recent times. Achieving this commitment will require concerted international cooperation.

At the time of this writing, the prospects for establishing an independent Palestinian state are uncertain. U.S. attention, without which a negotiated settlement between Palestinians and Israelis seems unlikely, has been focused primarily on Iraq. Nevertheless, a critical mass of Palestinians and Israelis—as well as the United States, Russia, the European Union, and the United Nations—remains committed to the goal of establishing a Palestinian state. And recent events, including the death of Yasser Arafat and the election of Mahmoud Abbas as his replacement, may yet turn this eventuality into a more imminent reality.

Our analyses are motivated by a firm belief that thoughtful preparation can facilitate peace. Certainly, when peace comes, such preparation will be essential to the success of the new state, as recent U.S. experience in Iraq and Afghanistan illustrates. The vision described in this book should help Palestinians, Israelis, and the international community prepare for the moment when the parties are ready to create and sustain a successful Palestinian state.

Figure Credits

Figure 1: Photo courtesy United States Agency for International Development (USAID), *Asalah Magazine*, No. 3, July 2003

Figure 2: Map courtesy Suisman Urban Design

Figure 3: Figure courtesy Suisman Urban Design

Figure 4: Figure courtesy Suisman Urban Design

Figure 5: Figure courtesy Suisman Urban Design

Figure 6: (left to right) Photos courtesy The Colorado Sprawl Action Center; Baron Wolman; Aga Khan Trust for Culture; Archivision; Aga Khan Trust for Culture

Figure 7: Photo courtesy Baron Wolman

Figure 8: Photo courtesy Baron Wolman

Figure 9: Map courtesy Suisman Urban Design

Figure 10: Figure courtesy Suisman Urban Design

Figure 11: Map courtesy Suisman Urban Design

Figure 12: Maps courtesy Suisman Urban Design

Figure 13: Map courtesy Suisman Urban Design

Figure 14: Maps courtesy Suisman Urban Design

Figure 15: Map courtesy Suisman Urban Design

Figure 16a: Figures courtesy Suisman Urban Design

Figure 16b: Figures courtesy Suisman Urban Design

Figure 17: Figure courtesy Suisman Urban Design

Figure 18: (top to bottom, left to right) All figures courtesy Suisman Urban Design; photos courtesy Israel National Railway; Baron Wolman; Florida Power and Light; Suisman Urban Design; Baron Wolman

Figure 19: (top to bottom, left to right) Photo courtesy Engineering and Geologic Earthquake Research Group, Purdue University; photographers Mete Sozen, Arvid Johnson, Antonio Bobet; photo courtesy San Jose Water District; photo courtesy SNCF; photo courtesy Baron Wolman

Figure 20: Photo courtesy Dan Leone, The Lane Construction Corporation

Figure 21: Photo of Transmilenio, SA

Figure 22: Photo courtesy Simon Tulloch

Figures 23, 24, 25: Figures courtesy Suisman Urban Design

Figure 26: Photo courtesy Ministry of Defence Publishing House, 1995, by Duby Tal, Moni Haramati, Varda Raz

Figures 27, 28: Figures courtesy Suisman Urban Design

Figure 29: Figure courtesy Suisman Urban Design

Figure 30: Figure courtesy Suisman Urban Design

Figure 31: Photo courtesy Luc Boegly

Figure 32: (left to right) Photos courtesy Jose Gabriel Sterling; Suisman Urban Design

Figure 33: (top to bottom, left to right) Photos courtesy King Fahad Hospital, MEDAES Limited, Aga Khan Trust for Culture, Aga Khan Trust for Culture

Figure 34: (top to bottom) Photos courtesy Jose Gabriel Sterling; Volvo Bus Corporation

Figure 35: Photos courtesy Suisman Urban Design

Figure 36: (top to bottom, left to right) First four photos courtesy Pere Vidal i Domènech, Projecto Gishur 2002–2003; last two photos courtesy Aga Khan Trust for Culture

Figure 37: Figure courtesy Suisman Urban Design

Figure 38: Photos courtesy Aga Khan Trust for Culture

Figure 39: Rendering courtesy Suisman Urban Design

Figure 40: Photos courtesy Baron Wolman

Figure 41: Photo courtesy Dubai International Airport

Figure 42: Figures courtesy Suisman Urban Design

Figure 43: (left to right) Photos courtesy Danway Dubai; Suisman Urban Design

Figure 44: Figure courtesy Suisman Urban Design

Figure 45: Photo courtesy Suisman Urban Design